face2face

Intermediate Workbook

Nicholas Tims with **Chris Redston & Gillie Cunningham**

CAMBRIDGE UNIVERSITY PRESS
Cambridge, New York, Melbourne, Madrid, Cape Town, Singapore, São Paulo, Delhi

Cambridge University Press
The Edinburgh Building, Cambridge CB2 8RU, UK

www.cambridge.org
Information on this title: www.cambridge.org/9780521676847

First published 2006
5th printing 2008

Printed in Dubai by Oriental Press

A catalogue record for this publication is available from the British Library

ISBN 978-0-521-67684-7 Workbook with Key
ISBN 978-0-521-60336-2 Student's Book with CD-ROM/Audio CD
ISBN 978-0-521-67685-4 Teacher's Book
ISBN 978-0-521-60340-9 Class Audio CDs
ISBN 978-0-521-60344-7 Class Audio Cassettes
ISBN 978-0-521-61398-9 Network CD-ROM
ISBN 978-0-521-69167-3 Intermediate and Upper Intermediate DVD
ISBN 978-8-483-23369-6 Student's Book with CD-ROM/Audio CD, Spanish edition
ISBN 978-3-125-39743-9 Student's Book with CD-ROM/Audio CD, Klett edition

Contents

Acknowledgements

Nicholas Tims would like to thank everyone at Cambridge and Pentacor for all their hard work, in particular Sue Ullstein (Commissioning Editor), Rachel Jackson-Stevens, Andrew Reid (Editors) and Linda Matthews (Production Editor) for their invaluable editorial and production skills. He would also like to thank Chris Redston, Gillie Cunningham, Clare Turnbull and Pat Tims for their encouragement and inspiration.

The authors and publishers would like to thank the following teachers for the invaluable feedback which they provided: Fernando Alba, Spain; Kevin Rutherford, Poland

The authors and publishers are grateful to the following contributors:
pentacor**big**: cover and text design and page make-up
Hilary Luckcock: picture research

The authors and publishers are grateful to the following for permission to reproduce copyright material. All efforts have been made to contact the copyright holders of material reproduced in this book which belongs to third parties, and citations are given for the sources. We welcome approaches from any copyright holders whom we have not been able to trace but who find that their material has been reproduced herein.
For the text on p23: Pascale Harter, adapted from 'Trying the Saharan sand cure', BBC News, www.bbc.news.co.uk; for the text on p43: Sue Flood, adapted from 'Filming killer whales hunting grey whales' *BBC Wildlife Magazine*, April 1999, www.bbc.co.uk/nature; for the text on p58: Nkem Ifejika, adapted from 'Confessions of a parking attendant' BBC News, bbc.news.co.uk.

The publishers are grateful to the following for permission to reproduce copyright photographs and material:

Key: l = left, c = centre, r = right, t = top, b = bottom

Advertising Archives for p33 (t); Alamy Images/©Photofusion PL for page 58; Ardea/©Francois Gohier for page 43; Bubbles/Angela Hampton for page 15, /Chris Rout for page 32; Camera Press/Stephen Mansfield/TSPL for page 48 (l); Channel 4/RDF Media for page 48 (r); Corbis/©Royalty Free for page 5 (l), /©Bettmann for page 20 (tr), /©Jules Perrier for page 50; Getty Images for pages 10 (t), 17, 23 and 64; Image State/Dave Houser for page 16; Photolibrary.com/ Photononstop for page 5 (r); Punchstock/Image Source for page 10 (b), /StockDisc for page 13; PhotoDisc for page 31, /Comstock for page 33 (b), /Brand X for page 49, /Bananastock for page 60, /Digital Vision for page 74; Rex for pages 20 (l), 20 (br), 28 and 63; Science Photo Library/NASA for page 41.

The publishers would like to thank the following illustrators:

Fred Blunt (Joking Apart), Mark Duffin, Joanne Kerr (New Division), Naf (Joking Apart), Jacquie O'Neill

1A Be happy!

Weekend activities V1.1

1 a) Which words/phrases do <u>not</u> go with the verbs?

1 go *clubbing/for a walk/(exhibitions)*
2 have *a quiet night in/the house/a lie-in*
3 visit *friends/relatives/to people online*
4 do *relatives/some gardening/some exercise*

b) Match the incorrect words/phrases in **1a)** to these words/phrases to make four more weekend activities.

~~go to~~   chat   visit   tidy up

1 *go to exhibitions*
2 *~~go to~~ chat to people online*
3 *visit relatives*
4 *tidy up a lie-in* ?

Question forms G1.1

2 Make questions with these words.

a) house / you / at weekends / tidy up / Do / your ?

   Do you tidy up your house at weekends?

b) been / in / the / you / last / clubbing / month / Have ?
   Have you been clubbing in the last month?

c) quiet / having / you next / When / a / night / in / are ?
   When are

d) round / you / have / How often / do / for dinner / people ?
   How often do you have people round for dinner?

e) people / online / ever / Have / chatted / you / to ?
   Have you ever chatted online to people online

f) you / a / have / Did / last weekend / lie-in ?
   Did you have a lie-in last weekend!

g) friends / visiting / you / weekend / this / Are / or relatives ?
   Are you visiting friends or relatives this weekend?

h) many / How / last year / go / did / you / exhibitions / to ?
   How many exhibitions did you go to last year

3 Read the article and write a question from **2** in the correct places 1–5.

Megan

Karen and Andy

Weekends **in** or weekends **out** ?

[1]How often do you have people round for dinner?

MEGAN Never. But last month I ate out with friends at least five times.

KAREN About once a month. My husband always cooks. This weekend we're visiting friends for dinner.

2

MEGAN I haven't had a quiet night in since I was a teenager!

ANDY Next Friday. We always have a quiet night in on Fridays.

3

MEGAN Yes, of course. Sunday mornings are perfect for lie-ins!

KAREN No! Lie-ins are impossible with two young children.

4

MEGAN Yes, I have. My brother lives abroad and it's cheaper than phoning.

KAREN The children chat to their friends online, but I haven't tried it yet.

5

MEGAN No, but I'm looking forward to going next week. It's my best friend's birthday.

ANDY The last time I went to a club it was called a disco and I was about 18!

4 **a)** Complete the questions with an auxiliary if necessary.

1 How many times _did_ Megan eat out last month?

2 Who _____ cooks when Karen and Andy have friends round for dinner?

3 When _____ Megan last have a quiet night in?

4 How often _____ Karen and Andy have quiet nights in?

5 Why _____ Karen and Andy never have lie-ins?

6 Why _is_ Megan going clubbing next week?

7 How many clubs _has_ Andy been to in the last year?

8 Who _____ chatted to people online at the weekend?

b) Answer the questions in **4a)**.

1 _She ate out with friends at least five times._

2 _Andy always cooks_

3 _She hasn't been having a quiet night for ages_

4 _Once a month_

5 _Because they have two children_

6 _It's her friends birthday_

7 _He's been none_

8 _____

1B Love it or hate it

Likes and dislikes V1.2

1 **a)** Match beginnings of sentences 1–8 to endings a)–h).

1 I'm very interested _e)_

2 I'm quite _a_

3 I don't _b_

4 I don't like going _h_

5 Tidying up my house _i_

6 I think lie-ins _i_

7 I'm not very keen _h_

8 I can't stand _d_

9 I enjoy having _d_

a) keen on joining my local gym.

b) mind going food shopping.

c) working at weekends.

d) a quiet night in.

e) in working abroad.

f) to the dentist at all.

g) drives me crazy.

h) on takeaway food.

i) at the weekends are wonderful.

b) Match the sentences in **1a)** to A–C.

A phrases to say you like something:
_1_ , _2_ , _6_ , _9_

B phrases to say something is OK:
_3_

C phrases to say you don't like something:
_4_ , _5_ , _7_ , _8_

Positive and negative verb forms, words and phrases G1.2

2 Read Martin's opinion of computers and fill in the gaps. Choose a), b) or c).

There aren't many things I ¹ _don't like_ in life, but computers drive me crazy. Of course, **everyone** ² _says_ they are a wonderful invention and we've got one at home for the children. **Both of them** ³ _have used_ a computer since they ⁴ _were_ young and they **hardly ever** ⁵ _had_ any problems. But when I ⁶ _tried_ to send an email or use the Internet, it **never** works properly. I ⁷ _'m not making_ excuses – I know it's my problem rather than the computer's. **None of** my friends like computers so maybe it ⁸ _'s_ something to do with our age. **I don't think** we'll ever understand them.

1 a) 'm not liking   (b) don't like   c) didn't like

2 a) says   b) said   c) is saying

3 a) are using   b) use   c) have used

4 a) have been   b) are   c) were

5 a) have   b) had   c) are having

6 a) tried   b) 'm trying   c) try

7 a) haven't made   b) didn't make   c) 'm not making

8 a) has been   b) was   c) 's

3 Now read Diane's opinion of computers and fill in the gaps with the correct form of the verbs in brackets. Use the Present Simple, Present Continuous, Past Simple or Present Perfect Simple.

I think computers are amazing. We ¹ _'ve had_ (have) one in our family for almost 20 years – since I ² _was_ (be) about 12. At that time we ³ _didn't use_ (not use) it for anything serious – **no one** did. My sister and I **usually** played games on it. Then at university I **always** ⁴ _wrote_ (write) my essays on it and I soon realised **there are lots of** things a computer can help with. Since then I ⁵ _'m not_ (not be able to) leave it alone! **All of** my friends ⁶ _call_ (call) me with their computer problems. I ⁷ _'ve not got_ (not get) paid or anything – I just do it as a favour. I ⁸ _'m helping_ (help) two of my friends with their computers at the moment – they're broken. **Neither of them** know anything about computers, but they know how to take me out for a meal!

4 Match these phrases in **bold** in 2 with their opposites in **bold** in 3.

1 There aren't many _there are lots of_
2 everyone _no one_
3 Both of them _neither of them_
4 hardly ever _always usually_
5 never _always_
6 None of _all of_
7 I don't think _I think_

5 Make these sentences positive or negative by changing the <u>underlined</u> words.

1 I <u>hardly ever</u> send emails from home.
I usually send emails from home.

2 He <u>thinks</u> the computer's got a virus.
He doesn't think ...

3 I <u>understood everything</u> he said.
I understood nothing ...

4 We <u>never used</u> our computer to do serious things.
We always used ...

5 <u>There aren't many</u> computers at my school.
There are lots of ...

6 Joe's <u>repaired</u> my laptop.
Joe's broken ...

7 <u>None of</u> my colleagues can type quickly.
All of ...

8 <u>Neither of</u> our parents can use computers.
Both of ...

9 He works with computers all day so he <u>doesn't need</u> one at home.
he needs

10 We <u>aren't using</u> the latest software.
are using

Review: verb forms

6 Correct the mistake in each sentence.

        drive
1 My parents ~~drives~~ me crazy at times.
2 I'm going ~~swimming~~ _to swim_ about three times a week.
3 Who ~~does~~ works with you?
4 How many countries have you ~~gone to~~ _been in?_
5 ~~In the past I~~ _I use to_ walk to school.
6 I ~~am~~ think you are correct.
7 I'm playing ~~a lot of~~ _a lot_ tennis in my free time.
8 I live in London for three years and I ~~love~~ _loved_ it.
9 I've been ~~to~~ _in_ Brazil last year.
10 Who ~~does~~ they work with?

Adjectives to describe feelings V1.3

1 Read the sentences. Complete the puzzle with adjectives to describe how the people are feeling.

1 She works really hard, but she can't get promotion.
2 He's forgotten his best friend's birthday.
3 She's got her driving test this afternoon.
4 He's just come back from a long holiday.
5 He didn't get the birthday present he wanted.
6 They don't understand the exercise.
7 Their son got the job he was applying for.
8 She hasn't got time to do everything she needs to do.

↓
1 F R U S T R A T E D
2 E
3 E
4 L
5 I
6 N
7 G
8 S

Reading: prepositions with adjectives V1.4

2 **a)** Read the article and choose the correct prepositions.

The funniest jokes in the world?

A recent experiment in the UK attempted to discover the world's funniest jokes. Dr Richard Wiseman from the University of Hertfordshire invited people from all over the world to send in their funniest jokes and rate* the jokes sent in by other people. In the year of the experiment, the website received over 40,000 jokes and 2 million ratings*!

The experiment showed many things about what different nationalities find funny. Many European countries, such as France and Denmark, preferred jokes about things we normally worry ¹*about/with/of* – for example, death, illness and marriage. Americans and Canadians liked jokes where someone was better ²*in/of/at* something than someone else. Germans, in particular, seem to be keen ³*at/on/about* jokes. Overall they gave jokes the highest scores.

Of course, there is a serious reason for the research. Dr Wiseman is interested ⁴*in/on/at* how we communicate. And humour and laughing are important parts of communication. Dr Wiseman was very pleased ⁵*of/with/at* the results.

He said the popular jokes seem to have three elements: a stressful situation, we feel superior to someone in the joke and we are surprised ⁶*of/by/in* something in the joke. Many of the jokes contained all three elements. For example, here is one of the most popular jokes:

> *Two men are playing golf one day. While they are playing they see a funeral procession* passing along the road nearby. One of the golfers stops, takes his cap off his head and closes his eyes. His friend says: "Wow, that is the nicest, sweetest thing I have ever seen. You really are a kind man." The first man answers: "Yeah, well, we were married for 35 years."*

*rate = give something a score (out of ten, for example)
*rating = the score you give something
**funeral procession* = the line of people taking a dead body on its last journey

b) Are these sentences true (T), false (F) or the text doesn't say (DS)?

1 [T] The experiment used the Internet.
2 [DS] The experiment lasted 12 months.
3 [F] The experiment only involved Europeans.
4 [F] The experiment was just for fun.
5 [DS] French people generally found jokes less funny than Danish people.
6 [T] German people generally found jokes funnier than other nationalities.
7 [F] Dr Wiseman felt the experiment was unsuccessful.

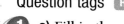

1D At a barbecue

Question tags RW1.1

1 a) Fill in the gaps with *not* and the correct form of the auxiliaries *do*, *be* or *have*.

1 You _aren't_ coming tomorrow.

2 I _don't_ need to bring anything to the barbecue.

3 Clare _didn't_ eat beef.

4 He _hasn't_ been here before.

5 They _haven't_ got any children.

6 We _didn't_ see him yesterday.

7 It _is_ going to rain.

8 You _haven't_ told him yet.

b) Write the sentences in 1a) next to the correct question tags a)–h).

a) _You aren't coming tomorrow_ , are you?

b) _It isn't going to rain_ , is it?

c) _They haven't got any children_ , have they?

d) _We didn't see him yesterday_ , did we?

e) _He hasn't been here before_ , has he?

f) _You haven't told him yet_ , have you?

g) _Clare didn't eat beef_ , does she?

h) _I don't need to bring anything to the barbecue_ , do I?

2 Write question tags for these sentences.

1 You eat fish, _don't you_ ?

2 You're vegetarian, _aren't you_ ?

3 Children love barbecues, _don't they_ ?

4 They came round for dinner once, _didn't they_ ?

5 He's being very sociable, _hasn't he_ ?

6 Their garden is looking very nice, _isn't it_ ?

7 I've cooked too much food, _haven't I_ ?

8 We've got a barbecue like yours, _haven't we_ ?

3 Change these questions into positive (+) or negative (–) statements with question tags.

1 Is she a teacher? (+) _She's a teacher, isn't she?_

2 Are they married? (–) _They aren't married, are they?_

3 Are we going home soon? (+) We are going home soon, aren't we?

4 Have you met our neighbours? (–) You haven't met our neighbours, have you?

5 Did you drive here? (–) You didn't drive here, do you?

6 Is it warm outside? (+) It's warm, outside, isn't it?

7 Does he want something to eat? (+) he wants something to eat, doesn't want?

8 Do you know Sam? (–) you don't know Sam, do you?

9 Has he got the address? (+) He's got the address, hasn't he?

10 Have you ever tried English sausages? (+) You've ever tried English sausages, haven't you?

11 Is he working this weekend? (–) He isn't working this weekend, is he?

12 Am I late? (–) I'm not late, am I?

Review: common mistakes

4 Correct the mistake in each sentence.

1 I'm really ~~interesting~~ *interested* in gardening.

2 Everyone ~~want~~ wants to go clubbing tonight.

3 ~~Their~~ They are going to have a lie-in tomorrow.

4 I often ~~loose~~ against my brother when we play tennis.

5 He's worked here for the year before last.

6 I've gone to France and I ~~thought~~ think it was beautiful.

7 I can't bear Paul and Sallys' dog.

8 Nobody ~~doesn't~~ wants want to come.

 Reading and Writing Portfolio 1 p64

2 We haven't got time

Language Summary 2, Student's Book p116

2A Slow down!

Work collocations V2.1

1 Put sentences a)–j) in the correct order.

Do you live to work ... or work to live?

a) **1** Count the hours! Do you spend more than

b) ☐ long hours? And weekends? Do you often take

c) **4** long hours is an early sign you might be

d) ☐ work home with you or regularly work

e) **6** some time off. It's good for you!

f) **4** to meet deadlines and sometimes everyone is

g) **2** 50 hours at work every week? Do you work

h) ☐ a few hours overtime? Of course, everyone has

i) **5** a workaholic. Find time to plan a holiday and take

j) **3** under pressure at work. But working

Modal verbs (1); *be able to, be allowed to, be supposed to* G2.1

2 Read the conversation and choose the correct verb form.

JAKE I'm really fed up with work.

KAY Why? You ¹(*don't have to*)/*mustn't* take work home like me.

JAKE I know, but I ²*'m able to*/*have to* work long hours and we're not ³*allowed*/*supposed* to be paid overtime.

KAY You aren't paid overtime! You ⁴*ought*/*'re supposed* to speak to your boss about that.

JAKE I know. I ⁵*should*/*can* ask him about a promotion, too.

KAY Are you ⁶*allowed*/*supposed* to work flexible hours?

JAKE Yes, but we're ⁷*allowed*/*supposed* to be at work between ten and four.

KAY And what about working at home? ⁸*Can*/*Must* you do that?

JAKE We ⁹*'re allowed to*/*must* work at home – but we have to ask our manager first. But I won't ¹⁰*be able to*/*can* work at home until I get my own flat.

KAY Well, you ¹¹*must*/*'re able to* start saving!

JAKE Yes, I know. I think I'm just a bit bored.

KAY Most work isn't interesting, I'm afraid. You ¹²*can*/*ought* to know that by now!

3 Rewrite these sentences with the words in brackets.

1 My advice is to ask for a promotion. (should)
   You *should ask for a promotion.*

2 If I were you, I'd take a week off. (ought)
   You ~~ought take a week off~~

3 I can't meet you tonight. (not be able to)
   I ~~'m not be able to meet you tonight~~

4 It's against the rules to work at weekends. (allowed)
   You ~~aren't allowed to work at weekend~~

5 It isn't necessary to wear a tie. (not have to)
   You ~~don't have to wear a tie~~

6 It's necessary to arrive before 9 a.m. (must)
   You ~~must arrive before 9 am~~

7 The company should give us holiday pay. (be supposed to)
   The company ~~is supposed to give us a holiday pay~~

8 You aren't allowed to leave work before 4 p.m. (mustn't)
   You ~~mustn't leave work before 4 pm~~

3 The tourist trade

Language Summary 3, Student's Book p119

3A Your holiday, my job

Phrasal verbs (1): travel V3.1

1 Read the conversation. Replace the phrases in **bold** with a phrasal verb from the box in the correct form.

~~look forward to~~   see (somebody) off   get around
put up with   pick (somebody) up   check into
set off   get back

Are you looking forward to

MUM ¹**Are you excited about** tomorrow?

CASS Of course. We're ²**leaving** very early, though.

MUM I know. I still want to come to the airport to
³**say goodbye to you**.

CASS Of course. Thanks, Mum.

MUM And give me a quick call when you⁴**'ve arrived
at** the hotel.

CASS Sure. Are you going to miss me?

MUM A bit. But at least I won't have to ⁵**tolerate**
your loud music.

CASS And you won't have to give me lifts so I can
⁶**travel about**.

MUM No. That's true. So what time do you
⁷**return**?

CASS At one o'clock in the morning.

MUM That's late!

CASS I know. So I was wondering ... can you
⁸**meet me** in the car?

Present Perfect Simple G3.1

2 Fill in the gaps in conversations 1–6 with the verbs in brackets. Use the Present Perfect Simple.

1 A Shirley _hasn't been_ (not go) abroad.

   B You're joking! Not even to France?

2 A _____ you ever _____ (work) in
      tourism?

   B Yes, I was a waiter in a hotel a long time ago.

3 A You _____ never _____ (bring)
      me back anything from your holidays.

   B Yes, I have! I gave you a picture of Venice once.

4 A Wow! You two have got a good suntan.

   B Yes. We _____ just _____
      (get back) from two weeks in the Caribbean.

5 A Hi, can I speak to Pat or Harry Skilton please?

   B Let's see. I'm afraid they _____
      (not check into) the hotel yet.

6 A The passengers are angry about the late flights.

   B I know. I _____ already _____
      (deal) with three complaints today.

3 Are sentences 1–9 correct? Change the incorrect sentences.

've known

1 I ~~knew~~ him since I was young.

2 Wendy and Carl never saw our old house.

3 We've run a bed and breakfast since three years.

4 I like your house. How long did you live here?

5 Mark isn't here. He's been to work.

6 We've set off hours ago, but we're stuck in traffic.

7 We haven't had a holiday this year.

8 Did you check into the hotel yet?

9 No one has picked me up at the airport.

4 Fill in the gaps with the Past Simple or Present Perfect Simple of the verbs in brackets.

José Guerreiro is a head chef in a restaurant for 1,000 people. But it's not a normal restaurant. It's open for breakfast, lunch and dinner, and it's always full.

José Guerreiro trained as a chef in Goa, India and ¹ _spent_ (spend) seven years working in restaurants in Indian cities. Then he saw an advertisement which changed his life.

"I ² _____ (always love) travelling so this seemed perfect," said José. He was offered the job and it ³ _____ (not take) him long to make his decision. Six months later he started work on a cruise ship, *The Sea Princess*.

15 years later, José is Head Chef on the same ship. "I ⁴ _____ (work) on four ships since I ⁵ _____ (join) the company.

But this is the first time I ⁶ _____ (be) Head Chef on a cruise. I ⁷ _____ (never feel) so nervous in my life!"

José shouldn't be nervous. In over 20 years as a chef he guesses he ⁸ _____ (learn) cooking styles from over 20 countries. "I can't think of anything I ⁹ _____ (not cook). I ¹⁰ _____ (deal with) every kind of special diet you can think of!" he laughed. "We had one passenger who ¹¹ _____ (not can) eat meat, fish, milk products or bread!"

I saw José again at the end of the first week. I asked him "What ¹² _____ we _____ (eat) so far, José?"

"So far, you ¹³ _____ (drink) 5,000 litres of milk and 150 kg of coffee. We ¹⁴ _____ (roast) about 1,000 chickens and made over 300 birthday and anniversary cakes. And no one ¹⁵ _____ (complain) yet!"

3B **Lonely Planet**

Phrases with *travel*, *get* and *go on*

V3.2

1 **a)** Fill in gaps 1–3 with these verbs.

| ~~travel~~ | get | go on |

b) Fill in gaps a)–f) with these words/phrases.

~~together~~	taxi to work
on your own	a journey
a cruise	out of a car

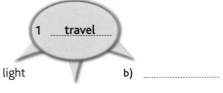

1 ___travel___

light

b) _____

a) ___together___

2 _____

a trip

c) _____

d) _____

3 _____

on a bus

e) _____

f) _____

Present Perfect Continuous and Present Perfect Simple G3.2

 2 Make sentences in the Present Perfect Continuous with *for* or *since*.

1 They started going on cruises three years ago.

They've been going on cruises for three years.

2 Marta started giving guided tours when she was 16.

_____

3 I started looking forward to my holiday six months ago.

_____

4 Cambridge University Press published its first book in 1584.

_____

5 We started going out together when I was 18.

_____

6 You moved into this house two months ago.

_____

 3 Choose the correct words. Sometimes both verb forms are possible.

 Philip Martin has never ¹*had/been having* a permanent home. He's ²*travelled/been travelling* round the world since he left university. "There are over 190 countries in the world and I've ³*stayed/been staying* in about 85 of them," he told me. At the moment he's in the Gambia in Africa. Unfortunately Philip hasn't ⁴*felt/been feeling* well for the last week. "I've ⁵*tried/been trying* a lot of different foods on my travels and I've never ⁶*had/been having* any problems before. But everyone has ⁷*looked after/been looking after* me very well!"

For the last ten years Philip has ⁸*kept/been keeping* a diary of his travels and so far he's ⁹*published/been publishing* two books about his adventures. Since he started writing, Philip hasn't ¹⁰*had/been having* to do other work. He's just ¹¹*finished/been finishing* his third book and he's now planning his journey to South America. "I've ¹²*explored/been exploring* this world for over 15 years, but I've got a long way to go!"

 4 Write questions with these words. Use the Present Perfect Simple or Present Perfect Continuous.

1 How long / Jane / wait?

How long has Jane been waiting?

2 How many cruises / you / go / on?

How many cruises have you been on?

3 How many hotels / you / work / in?

_____

4 How many times / you / go / on a package holiday?

_____

5 How long / he / take / work home?

_____

6 How many times / you / get / a taxi to work?

_____

7 How long / you / study / English?

_____

8 How long / Tony and Maureen / be / married?

_____

 5 Fill in the gaps with the correct form of the verbs in brackets. Use the Present Perfect Continuous if possible.

1 We *'ve been watching* (watch) a lot of travel programmes recently.

2 Why didn't you call me? How _____ you _____ (get around) with a broken leg?

3 We _____ (not go) on a guided tour of the city before, so we'd like to go.

4 The sun _____ (shine) all weekend. It's wonderful!

5 I _____ (go) on package holidays for years and I've never had any problems.

6 Lindsay _____ (not take) any time off this year. She works so hard.

7 _____ you _____ (know) each other for long?

8 I _____ (not travel) first class before and I'm quite excited about it.

9 Who is he? He _____ (stand) outside for hours.

Word formation (1): suffixes for adjectives and nouns V3.3

1 Complete the table with the adjectives or nouns.

	adjective	noun
1	adventurous	*adventure*
2	dangerous	
3		enormity
4		importance
5	sad	
6		seriousness
7	famous	
8	modest	
9	accidental	

2 Read the article. Choose the best answers.

1 Alan is from …

   a) Nepal. **b)** the UK. c) Japan.

2 Alan Hinkes has climbed …

   a) Everest 14 times.

   b) 14 mountains in Nepal and Pakistan.

   c) the 14 tallest mountains in the world.

3 Alan climbs mountains because …

   a) he loves doing it.

   b) he doesn't like teaching any more.

   c) he gets a lot of money for it.

4 Alan hurt his back …

   a) in a snowstorm.

   b) because he sneezed.

   c) when he fell.

5 To pay for his trips, Alan …

   a) speaks about his adventures.

   b) makes films about climbing.

   c) both a) and b).

6 In his country, Alan is …

   a) very well-known.

   b) a hero to some people.

   c) a schoolteacher.

3 Read the article again and fill in gaps 1–9 with an adjective or noun from 1.

Climb every mountain ...

NAME	HEIGHT (m)	NAME	HEIGHT (m)
EVEREST	8,850	MANASLU	8,163
K2	8,611	NANGA PARBAT	8,125
KANGCHENJUNGA	8,586	ANNAPURNA	8,091
LHOTSE	8,516	GASHERBRUM I	8,068
MAKALU	8,463	BROAD PEAK	8,047
CHO OYU	8,201	GASHERBRUM II	8,035
DHAULAGIRI	8,167	SHISHA PANGMA	8,013

There is a popular saying in Japanese: "There are two kinds of fool*. Those who never climb Mount Everest and those who do it twice."

So what is Alan Hinkes? An ¹**a** *dventurous* fool perhaps? This 51-year-old former geography teacher has climbed all 14 of the world's highest mountains. More people have landed on the moon than have tried this extremely ²**d**_____ achievement.

The world's tallest mountains are all in Nepal and Pakistan. They are over 8,000 metres high. At this height helicopters cannot rescue people and the physical demands are ³**e**_____ . When you finally reach the top of a mountain, there's no time to celebrate – it's ⁴**i**_____ to remember that you have to get down the mountain again.

Alan's been climbing mountains since he was teenager. "I'm addicted to it," he says. However, there has been some ⁵**s**_____ in his adventures. In 1995 he was climbing K2 with his close friend Alison Hargreaves. Near the top, they separated and Alan continued to climb alone. Alison and six other people later died in a snowstorm.

One of Alan's most ⁶**s**_____ injuries on a mountain was rather unusual. He was eating a chapati – a type of Indian bread – when the flour got up his nose and he sneezed*. He injured his back and had to be rescued by helicopter.

Despite his amazing achievement, Hinkes is not ⁷**f**_____ . His ⁸**m**_____ means that people remember him more for the chapati ⁹**a**_____ than the mountains he's climbed. Each trip costs him about £30,000 and he raises the money by giving talks and selling videos of his climbs. Now, many people want him to receive a knighthood* from the Queen. Perhaps the 'fool' Alan Hinkes will soon be Sir Alan Hinkes …

*fool = stupid person
*sneeze = when you sneeze, air comes out of your nose and mouth in a way you can't control
*knighthood = an award from the Queen of England for doing something special

3D A trip to India

Review: prepositions with adjectives

1 Choose the correct preposition. Sometimes more than one answer is possible.

1 I'm feeling very nervous (of)/(about)/at the flight next week. I'm really scared *with/of/at* flying.

2 I'm fed up *by/with/on* my husband's snoring and he gets annoyed *about/with/of* me when I wake him up.

3 The manager didn't seem concerned *with/about/by* our worries and we were so angry *at/on/with* him that we checked out early.

4 Nikki was very upset *of/by/about* splitting up with Mark, but she told me she was fed up *of/at/with* him going out every night.

Asking for and making recommendations RW3.1

2 **a)** Make questions with these words.

1 know / Do / any good / stay / places / to / you ?

   Do you know any good places to stay?

2 anything / worth / Is / seeing here / there ?

   ----

3 tips / got / other / Have / you / any ?

   ----

4 near / about / sea / places / What / the ?

   ----

5 place / a / the / to / What's / best / car / hire ?

   ----

b) Complete the conversations with the sentences in **1a)**.

1 A   _Do you know any good places to stay?_

   B   Sorry, no. But I wouldn't recommend anywhere near the station.

2 A   --

   B   I'd recommend one of the companies at the airport.

3 A   --

   B   Yes. You should definitely visit the cathedral.

4 A   --

   B   It isn't really worth going there. The beaches are quite dirty.

5 A   --

   B   Yes. You should learn a bit of the language. It really helps.

3 Fill in the gaps in the conversations with the phrases in the boxes.

| ~~are the best~~   's the best   'd recommend |
| sounds wonderful   wouldn't go   really useful |

1

ANN   You've been to India, Louise. What

   ¹ _are the best_ places to visit?

LOUISE   I ² _____ Kerala – in the south. Beautiful lakes, canals ... it's like paradise.

ANN   That ³ _____ . What

   ⁴ _____ time of year to visit?

LOUISE   Well, I ⁵ _____ between September and January. It can be really wet then.

ANN   That's ⁶ _____ .

| to know   bother   should go to |
| Do you know any   And is there |

2

ANN   ⁷ _____ good places to stay?

LOUISE   Yes, but don't ⁸ _____ booking in advance. It's cheaper to get a hotel there.

ANN   That's good ⁹ _____ .

   ¹⁰ _____ anything else worth visiting in the south?

LOUISE   Of course. India's a big place. If you like beaches, you ¹¹ _____ Goa.

| I've heard   And what about   You really must |
| It's probably best   Have you got any |

3

ANN   ¹² _____ money?

LOUISE   ¹³ _____ to take cash. Credit cards aren't very useful outside big cities.

ANN   Right. ¹⁴ _____ other tips?

LOUISE   Lots. ¹⁵ _____ visit one big city. Indian cities are just incredible.

ANN   Yes, ¹⁶ _____ that.

 Reading and Writing Portfolio 3 p68

4 Born to be wild

Language Summary 4, Student's Book p122

Riders

Music collocations V4.1

1 Fill in the gaps with the correct form of these verbs.

~~release~~   see   go (x 2)
play   appear   have

Nowadays the business of selling music is a little more complicated than simply ¹ _releasing_ a new album. Groups also have to promote their records so they have to ² .... on TV and talk about the new album. What's more, fans like ³ .... their favourite group play live so groups also have to ⁴ .... on tour. ⁵ .... onstage and ⁶ .... concerts every night is exhausting, but if you want to ⁷ .... an album in the charts, you have to promote it!

Past Simple and Past Continuous G4.1

2 Fill in the gaps with the verbs in brackets. Use the Past Simple or Past Continuous.

Seven things you didn't know about ... Rock and Pop

◆ In 1958, while Elvis ¹ __was earning__ (earn) $400,000 a month, he had to go into the army. His salary ² .... (go) down to $78 a month.

◆ In 1959, a teacher ³ .... (throw) a 16-year-old Jimi Hendrix out of school because he ⁴ .... (hold) the hand of a white girl in his class.

◆ In April 1964, while the Beatles ⁵ .... (finish) their second album, they ⁶ .... (have) hit records in all of the top 5 positions in the US charts.

◆ In 1963, Roy Orbison ⁷ .... (be) on tour with the Beatles. He ⁸ .... (wear) sunglasses because he couldn't find his glasses. He liked the look so much that for the rest of his career he only ⁹ .... (wear) sunglasses.

◆ In 1970, while the rock group Pink Floyd ¹⁰ .... (playing) in front of a large lake in London, the music ¹¹ .... (be) so loud that some of the fish in the lake ¹² .... (die).

◆ Sheryl Crowe ¹³ .... (lose) her two front teeth when she ¹⁴ .... (be) eight. Over 15 years later she ¹⁵ .... (sing) in a bar when a waitress accidentally ¹⁶ .... (hit) her with a glass. The same two front teeth ¹⁷ .... (fall) out.

◆ In 2000, while Madonna ¹⁸ .... (stay) in Sweden for the MTV Music Awards, she ¹⁹ .... (ask) the hotel to change the colour of the room. She ²⁰ .... (want) a 'calm colour' to help her meditate. Madonna ²¹ .... (not joke) and the hotel immediately ²² .... (paint) the room.

used to G4.2

3 Fill in the gaps with *used to* or the Past Simple of the verb in brackets. Use *used to* where possible.

Before they were famous ...

1 Madonna ___used to work___ (work) at Dunkin' Donuts. She __got__ (get) sacked for spilling jam on a customer.

2 When the rap singer P Diddy _____ (be) a teenager, he _____ (wash) cars and make tea at a record company.

3 Ricky Martin _____ (be) an actor on the American TV soap, *General Hospital*. After two years, Ricky decided he _____ (prefer) music to acting.

4 Elvis _____ (lose) his first job in a factory because he _____ (be) only 15. He _____ (earn) $30 a week there.

5 Britney Spears and Justin Timberlake _____ _____ (present) a children's TV programme called the *Mickey Mouse Club*.

6 Elton John _____ (not be) called 'Elton John'. In 1971, he _____ (change) his name because he wanted to be famous. What _____ his name _____ (be)? Reginald Dwight!

 4B **Adventurers**

Character adjectives V4.2

1 Choose the correct word.

1 He works long hours and never takes time off.
   a) ambitious   b) generous   c) (reliable)

2 They often go on holiday to places I've never heard of!
   a) organised   b) adventurous   c) ambitious

3 Tim gets embarrassed quite easily.
   a) sensitive   b) sensible   c) brave

4 My sister always brings me back a present from her holidays.
   a) reliable   b) practical   c) generous

5 I think he prefers to travel on his own.
   a) determined   b) independent   c) confident

6 Kathy will know what time the meeting is.
   a) practical   b) talented   c) organised

7 My boss always makes good decisions.
   a) sensitive   b) mean   c) sensible

8 They won't give up until they find the answer.
   a) determined   b) reliable   c) adventurous

Past Perfect G4.3

2 Fill in the gaps with the verbs in brackets in the Past Perfect. Use contractions if possible.

1 Connor __had arranged__ (arrange) to meet up with some friends so he couldn't come with us.

2 I really wanted to see the concert, but it _____ (sell out).

3 Simon _____ (not drive) abroad before, so he wasn't very confident.

4 I _____ (not hear) any of their music before, but I thought the gig was excellent.

5 By the time I arrived, everyone _____ (leave).

6 He failed the test because he _____ (not do) any revision.

7 When Jade arrived at the restaurant, she realised she _____ (go) there before.

8 They _____ (not know) each other for long when they decided to get engaged.

3 **a) Read the first part of Charlie's story and choose the correct words.**

By the time I was 18, I ¹*stopped/* *had stopped* going on holiday with my parents. The first year I ²*stayed/* *had stayed* at home, my parents asked me to pick them up at the airport. The night before they ³*got back/had got back*, I realised the house was a mess. I ⁴*didn't tidy up/* *hadn't tidied up* for two weeks. I finally went to bed about 3 a.m. and a few minutes later I ⁵*was/* *had been* fast asleep. I woke up suddenly at 7 a.m. I ⁶*arranged/* *had arranged* to meet them at the airport at 6.30 a.m. and I ⁷*didn't set/* *hadn't set* the alarm! I quickly set off for Heathrow airport, but there are four terminals at Heathrow airport and it's one of the biggest airports in the world! I had no idea which terminal they ⁸*arrived/* *had arrived* at! And this ⁹*was/had been* before the days of mobile phones ...

b) Tick three more events that happen in the story.

a) ✓ Charlie's parents asked him to pick them up at the airport.

b) ☐ Charlie tidied up the house.

c) ☐ Charlie set his alarm.

d) ☐ Charlie's parents arrived at the airport.

e) ☐ Charlie woke up.

f) ☐ Charlie phoned his parents.

 4 **a) Read the second part of the story and put the verbs in brackets in the Past Perfect or Past Simple.**

When I arrived at Terminal 1, I was an hour late. When I eventually found my parents at Terminal 3, they ¹ *had spent* (spend) two hours waiting for me. They ² .... (not be) pleased. They ³ .... (be) on a flight for 12 hours and they were exhausted. But things were getting worse ... when we ⁴ .... (get back) to the car, I realised I ⁵ .... (lose) my car keys somewhere at the airport. We phoned my elder brother and he came and took my parents home.

About three hours later, I ⁶ .... (get) home. Fortunately someone ⁷ .... (find) my keys at the airport. The first thing I ⁸ .... (see) was my father repairing a broken window. What had happened?

When my parents and my brother ⁹ .... (get) home, they realised they hadn't got any house keys. They ¹⁰ .... (have to) break a window to get into the house!

b) Put events a)–f) in the correct order 1–6.

a) ☐ 1 Charlie lost his keys.   d) ☐ Charlie met his parents.

b) ☐ Charlie's parents got home.   e) ☐ Charlie got home.

c) ☐ Charlie's parents broke a window.   f) ☐ Charlie's brother arrived at the airport.

Review: apostrophes

5 **Write the full form of 's and 'd if possible.**

1 It**'s** taken three hours to get here. *has*

2 I**'d** always thought he was sensible. *had*

3 He**'s** been living in London three years. ....

4 We**'d** recommend practical clothes for the journey. ....

5 It**'s** published by Cambridge University Press. ....

6 She**'d** never been skiing before. ....

7 They**'d** get home earlier if they didn't always drive. ....

8 It**'s** the first time Simon**'s** been to Scotland. ...., ...

9 I thought I**'d** enjoy the film because I**'d** loved the book. ...., ...

10 Paul**'s** brother**'s** always been ambitious. ...., ...

4C Natural medicines

Reading: guessing meaning from context V4.3

1 Read the article quickly. Complete the sentence. Choose a), b) or c).

The writer tried the sand cure ...

a) because he had health problems.

b) but didn't enjoy the experience.

c) and thought it was a positive experience.

2 a) Look at the words in **bold** in the article. Are they nouns, verbs or adjectives?

1 tribe   *noun*

2 gaining   ....

3 alleviates   ....

4 backs up   ....

5 peak   ....

6 scorching   ....

7 crunching   ....

8 measly   ....

b) Choose the correct meanings of the words in **2a)**.

1 **tribe**	a)	(group of people)	b)	group of animals
2 **gaining**	a)	increasing	b)	decreasing
3 **alleviates**	a)	doesn't help	b)	helps
4 **backs up**	a)	supports	b)	doesn't support
5 **peak**	a)	lowest point	b)	highest point
6 **scorching**	a)	very hot	b)	very cold
7 **crunching**	a)	chewing	b)	drinking
8 **measly**	a)	very large	b)	very small

3 Read the article again. Are these sentences true (T), false (F) or the article doesn't say (DS)?

1 [F] The sand cure is a modern natural cure.

2 [ ] The sand cure is only practised in the Saharan desert.

3 [ ] Tourists have been trying the sand cure.

4 [ ] The sand cure can help with stomach problems.

5 [ ] Local doctors don't think the sand cure is useful.

6 [ ] The writer tried the sand cure because he had had too much tea.

7 [ ] It's good to try the sand cure on windy days.

8 [ ] The writer spent less time in the sand than the Saharawi usually do.

Trying the Sahara sand cure

The Sahara Desert is one of the driest regions on earth. Very little grows in temperatures that can reach 57°C. So what could be healthy about this place? According to the Saharawi, a **tribe** who live in the desert in the Western Sahara, it has more than enough of what is needed: heat and sand*.

The Saharawi have been using the sand cure* for hundreds of years. And recently this treatment has been **gaining** popularity with tourists. My guide explained the technique: "We make a big hole, cover ourselves in lotion*, get in the hole and stay in the sun for a few hours."

The Saharawi believe the cure **alleviates** skin and back problems. And a local doctor **backs up** their claims. Dr Coulon has been a doctor in Morocco for more than 30 years and has tried the sand cure herself. "It's very good for your bones, muscles and circulation," she says.

So, after several cups of mint tea, I agreed to try the cure myself. At midday the heat is at its **peak** and you can hardly walk on the **scorching** sand. I started wishing for a cooling wind. Bad idea. The experience of being buried in sand is not unpleasant – it's a bit like a hot, dry bath. But the experience of **crunching** on sand in your mouth is not pleasant at all.

After 20 minutes I was so relaxed I felt I could stay there for ever. The desert is so quiet. But ten minutes later, my guides starting helping me out. I had spent a **measly** half an hour in the sand. The Saharawis spend two hours. My conclusions? Well, I certainly felt more relaxed and very clean – when I'd got all the sand out of my ears, nose and mouth, of course.

*sand = something found on beaches and in deserts
*cure = something that makes someone with an illness healthy again
*lotion = a liquid that you put on your skin to protect it

Adjectives to describe behaviour V4.4

1 Complete the puzzle with character adjectives.

```
          ¹E
          N
      ²B  T      ³V
      |   H      |
   ⁴R    U      |
   |     S      |
⁵A |     I      |
|  ⁶O    A      |
|  |     S      |
⁷S ⁸L    T      |
|  |     I      |
⁹L |     C      |
|
¹⁰L
```

People who ...

1 are very interested and involved in an activity.
2 become angry easily.
3 hurt or attack others.
4 aren't polite.
5 always think they are the best.
6 upset other people by their behaviour.
7 are selfish because they're allowed to do what they want.
8 will always support their friends.
9 don't like working.
10 make a lot of noise.

Softening opinions and making generalisations RW4.1

2 Match sentences 1–5 to the softer opinions in sentences a)–e) about professional football players.

1 They are selfish towards their younger team-mates.

   _d)_

2 They're often a bit stupid.

   ....

3 They train a lot. ....

4 They usually aren't violent people. ....

5 They think they know everything. ....

a) Some of them can be quite arrogant at times.
b) They tend to be rather hard-working.
c) On the whole, most of them aren't very intelligent.
d) They can be a bit inconsiderate towards young players.
e) Generally speaking, they aren't aggressive.

3 Correct the mistakes in the phrases in **bold**.

   quite helpful

1 She can be **helpful quite** at times.

2 **He tends being** rather noisy in class.

3 **On whole** most of our students are hard-working.

4 **General speaking,** my children are quite polite.

5 Some modern films can be a bit **violence**.

6 My teenage son can be **arrogant a bit**.

7 They can be rather **inpolite** at times.

8 A few football fans can be a bit **agressive**.

4 Use the words/phrases in brackets to soften these opinions about men and women.

MEN

1 They snore.
(Some of them / can / at times)

   Some of them can snore at times.

2 They are considerate.
(not very / at times)

   ....

   ....

3 They are untidy.
(Some of them / can / rather)

   ....

   ....

WOMEN

4 They are better with money.
(tend to / a bit)

   ....

   ....

5 Women like shopping.
(Generally speaking / most)

   ....

   ....

6 They are more organised than men.
(On the whole / tend to)

   ....

   ....

 Reading and Writing Portfolio 4 p70

5 Home truths

Language Summary 5, Student's Book p125

5A Moving house

Homes V5.1

1 Look at the pictures. Write the names.

Who lives in a …

1 semi-detached house? _Lisa and Mike_

2 detached house? ....

3 bungalow? ....

4 terraced house? ....

Sam

Lisa and Mike

The Stephens family

James and Mel

2 Do the puzzle. Find the type of house ().

A room or place …
1 outside the house.
2 at the top of the house.
3 where you work.
4 where you cook.
5 where you wash.
6 where the car is parked.
7 at the bottom of the house.

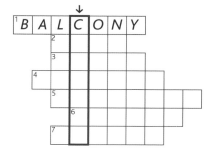

| ¹B | A | L | C | O | N | Y |

Making comparisons G5.1

3 Look at the advertisements and match the places to sentences 1–8. Write P (Poplar), H (Hackney) or B (Bow).

Poplar	**Hackney**	**Bow**
3-bedroom semi-detached house (needs work) 120 square metres Built in 1910 **£230,000** Distance to underground: 10 mins	2-bedroom spacious terraced house 150 square metres Built in 1920 **£280,000** Distance to underground: 5 mins	NEW 3-bedroom flat 100 square metres **£250,000** Distance to underground: 7 mins

1 [H] It's far more spacious than the other two.

2 [ ] It's slightly cheaper than the Hackney house.

3 [ ] It isn't as big as the others.

4 [ ] It needs a lot more work than the other two.

5 [ ] It's a bit more expensive than the Bow flat.

6 [ ] It's a little older than the Hackney house.

7 [ ] It's slightly further from the underground than the Hackney house.

8 [ ] It's slightly closer to the underground than the Poplar house.

4 Glen and Bev went to see the three places. Fill in their comments with these words.

~~smallest~~	little	much less	similar
most	best	the least	far	as close

The Poplar house has got the ¹ _smallest_ garden I've ever seen.

It isn't ² .... to the underground as they said.

It's very ³ .... to our house.

The Bow flat is ⁴ .... interesting than the others.

It's ⁵ .... more modern than the other two.

It needs ⁶ .... work of the three.

The Hackney house feels a ⁷ .... lighter than the other three.

It's in the ⁸ .... neighbourhood.

It seems to be the ⁹ .... popular of the three.

5 Glen and Bev are making their decision. Fill in the gaps with the correct form of the adjectives.

GLEN   I hate doing this. Everything is so expensive.

BEV   Yes ... and then next year they'll be a bit
        [1] _more expensive_ (expensive)!

GLEN   OK. Well let's start with the flat. I know it's your
        [2] _____ (favourite) place.

BEV   Yes. But it's just not as [3] _____
        (interesting) as the other two.

GLEN   So, what about the house in Poplar? It's £50,000
        [4] _____ (cheap).

BEV   And it's probably got the [5] _____
        (character) of the three.

GLEN   But could we do all that work?

BEV   Well, you're one of the [6] _____
        (determined) people I know.

GLEN   Yes, but I'm no [7] _____ (good) at
        DIY than you.

BEV   So, the Hackney house. I know you thought this
        was the [8] _____ (light) of the
        three.

GLEN   But it's in the [9] _____ (busy) area.

BEV   And £280,000 is such a lot of money ...

GLEN   Yes, well it's a lot [10] _____
        (fashionable) round there than it used to be.

BEV   So are we any [11] _____ (far)
        towards making a decision?

GLEN   Not really. Let's sleep on it.

5B A load of old junk

Phrasal verbs (2) V5.2

1 Fill in the gaps with the correct form of these verbs.

~~clear~~	throw (x 2)		come	take
sort	give	tidy	put	go

1   I've been _clearing_ out the junk in the loft.

2   Have you _____ out which clothes you want
    to keep?

3   _____ your toys away – it's time for bed!

4   I'm _____ out these old CDs! Do you want any
    of them?

5   Don't forget to _____ through the pockets
    before you wash those trousers.

6   I don't want any money for the old sofa – I'm happy
    to _____ it away for nothing.

7   When are you going to _____ away those old
    newspapers?

8   Are you _____ back tonight or are you staying
    at your friend's house?

9   Have you _____ up the living room? It was a
    mess earlier.

10 The dentist said he'd have to _____ a tooth out.

The future G5.2

2 **a)** Match questions 1–5 to the best responses a)–e).

1   Why are you
    watching me?
    ___b)___

2   Have you asked your boss about promotion?
    _____

3   Is Tim there, please? _____

4   Have you decided what you want? _____

5   Why won't you lend him your laptop? _____

a) Wait a minute. I'll just check.
b) Because you're going to cut yourself.
c) Because he'll break it.
d) Yes. I'm going to have some lamb.
e) Not yet. I'm seeing him this afternoon.

b) **Match sentences a)–e) in 2a) to these uses of the future.**

1   a prediction ___c)___

2   a prediction based on present evidence _____

3   a decision made at the time of speaking _____

4   a plan to do something _____

5   an arrangement _____

3 Choose the correct words.

1 I (*'m leaving*)/*'ll leave* at five o'clock because I need to catch a train.

2 Don't tell my brother. He*'ll*/*'s going to* be furious.

3 I think this house *will*/*is going to* be worth a lot more in the future.

4 This traffic is terrible. We*'ll*/*'re going to* be very late.

5 We*'re looking*/*'ll look* at some houses on Saturday. Do you want to come?

6 A The kitchen is really dirty.
   B Is it? OK, I*'m sorting it out*/*'ll sort it out* later.

7 I*'m going to work*/*'m working* a lot harder for my next English exam.

4 There is one mistake in each of the conversations. Write the correct sentence.

1 A Are you to looking for a flat or a house?
   B We'll have to see what we can afford.

   Are you looking for a flat or a house?

2 A What you are going to do with all those old clothes?
   B I'll probably give them to charity.

   _____

3 A What are you doing later?
   B I'm play cards so I'll be back late.

   _____

4 A I heard you're moving to the country.
   B Yes, it's going be a big change.

   _____

5 A I'll calling you this evening about the meeting.
   B OK. But I'm going to bed early tonight so call before nine.

   _____

6 A Mum and Dad will be furious when they see this!
   B I'll to tidy it up before they come back.

   _____

5 Put the verbs in brackets in the correct form. Use the Present Continuous, *be going to* or *'ll* + infinitive. Sometimes more than one answer is possible.

1

RUTH Simon ¹ *'s having* (have) a birthday lunch on Sunday.

MEL I know. ² _____ you _____ (buy) him a present?

RUTH Yes. That's why I wanted to come to the market.

MEL Well, maybe we ³ _____ (find) something here.

RUTH It ⁴ _____ (be) hard. It's mainly a load of old junk.

2

ELLEN Do you think we ⁵ _____ (need) any of this stuff again?

JERRY Well, I ⁶ _____ definitely _____ (not listen) to any of these CDs.

ELLEN ⁷ _____ you _____ (give) them to charity?

JERRY Maybe. They cost me hundreds of pounds, though.
Wait. I've got an idea. I ⁸ _____ (sell) them on the Internet!

ELLEN Good idea. People ⁹ _____ (buy) anything on eBay.

3

BEN I ¹⁰ _____ (tidy) the flat this weekend. It's a mess.

PETE You're right. I ¹¹ _____ (not do) anything on Saturday. I ¹² _____ (help) you.

BEN Ah. I can't do it tomorrow. I'm really sorry. I ¹³ _____ (meet) Amy.

PETE OK. I ¹⁴ _____ (give) you a hand on Sunday then.

BEN Hmm. I ¹⁵ _____ (take) Amy to my parents on Sunday.

PETE So when ¹⁶ _____ you _____ (tidy) the flat then?

BEN OK. Maybe I ¹⁷ _____ (do) it next weekend. Are you free then?

VOCABULARY AND READING

Reading

1 Read the article quickly and decide which paragraph 1–5 is about these things.

a) IKEA's newest product in the UK. ___1___

b) The history of BoKlok housing. _____

c) The advantages of prefabs. _____

d) The history of prefabs in general. _____

e) How BoKlok housing is built. _____

2 Read the article again and complete the sentences with the meaning of these names and numbers.

1 IKEA *One of the companies working with BoKlok UK.*

2 12

   The minimum number _____

3 1998

   The year _____

4 Over 2,000

   The number of _____

5 Japan and the UK

   The countries where _____

   _____

Verb patterns (1) V5.3

3 Complete sentence b) so it has the same meaning as sentence a).

1 a) BoKlok makes it possible for low-income people to buy their own home.

   b) BoKlok allows *low-income people to buy their own home.*

2 a) It looks like prefabs are more popular nowadays.

   b) Prefabs seem _____

3 a) Over 2,000 people in Scandinavia have bought a BoKlok home.

   b) Over 2,000 people in Scandinavia have decided

   _____

4 a) In the future perhaps more people will live in prefabs.

   b) In the future more people might _____

5 a) Many people want to buy their own home.

   b) Many people would like _____

6 a) It doesn't bother me that I live with my parents.

   b) I don't mind _____

PREFABULOUS!

1 **IKEA is working with BoKlok UK to be part of a revolution in housing in the UK. BoKlok means 'Live Smart' and is a project to provide affordable homes to people on average incomes. It aims to build small communities of BoKlok housing with at least 12 flats, 6 in each block.**

2 So will you soon be able to go to IKEA and drive away with a new home? Well, no, you won't. BoKlok finds the land, gets permission to build, and the low-cost housing will only be available to people who can't afford their own home. The flats are built in a factory and delivered to the site – IKEA supply the kitchens and the bathrooms. Buyers can then choose furniture and get advice on interior design from IKEA.

3 BoKlok has been selling housing in Scandinavia since 1998 and the flats cost about 30% less than a normal flat. So far, BoKlok has sold over 2,000 homes – all of them in communities with shared facilities, such as gardens, to make neighbours socialise as much as possible.

4 Houses of this type are called prefabs* in the UK and the USA. And they're not a new idea. In the early 20th century, the large American shop, Sears, offered prefabs. In Japan and the UK after World War II, prefabs were a popular way of building new houses quickly and cheaply.

5 Nowadays the price of housing in many countries makes it very difficult for a lot of people to buy or even rent. Prefabs offer home-buyers modern, quality homes which are designed by architects and are often very environmentally efficient. In the USA the popularity of prefabs is growing rapidly with young people who want a 21st century-designed house.

*prefabs = short for prefabricated houses

5D Is this what you mean?

Materials V5.4

1 What is the main material usually used in these items?

| ~~rubber~~ plastic metal paper wool |
| cardboard wood glass cotton leather |

1 a tyre __rubber__
2 a mirror _____
3 shoes _____
4 socks _____
5 boxes _____
6 a ballpoint pen _____
7 a microwave oven _____
8 a jumper _____
9 a bookshelf _____
10 a magazine _____

Explaining what you need RW5.1

2 **a)** Match sentences 1–6 to pictures a)–f).

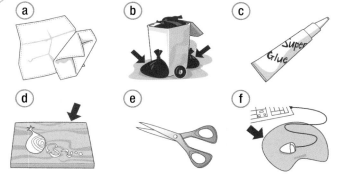

1 You use them to put rubbish in. __b)__
2 They're things for cleaning your mouth or hands when you're eating. _____
3 You use it when you want to cut vegetables. _____
4 They're things for cutting paper. _____
5 You use it to join two things when they are broken. _____
6 I'm looking for something for my computer. You use it under a mouse. _____

b) Match sentences 1–6 to pictures a)–f) in 2a).

1 They're made of metal. __e)__
2 It's a type of liquid. _____
3 They're made of paper or cotton. _____
4 It's made of wood or sometimes plastic. _____
5 They're made of plastic. _____
6 It's made of rubber. _____

3 Fill in the gaps in the conversations with the phrases in the boxes.

| ~~You use them~~ Do you mean it's made of |
| You mean the word for what they're called |
| They're usually It's stuff for |

JUAN ¹ _You use them_ to start a barbecue.

MAN ² _____ matches?

JUAN No, I'm sorry. I can't remember ³ _____ in English. ⁴ _____ white.

MAN Oh, you mean firelighters.

BIBI ⁵ _____ putting on food. I'm sorry, I don't know ⁶ _____ it.

MAN Do you mean salt?

BIBI No, ⁷ _____ plastic.

MAN Ah! ⁸ _____ clingfilm.

| ~~You use~~ You use them they're made of |
| What's it called you're looking for |
| I'm looking for It's a type of for cleaning |

MARIA ⁹ _You use_ it when you make a mistake. ¹⁰ _____ liquid.

WOMAN Is this what ¹¹ _____ ?

MARIA Yes, that's it. ¹² _____ in English?

WOMAN Tippex or correction fluid.

HUGO ¹³ _____ something for my shoes.

WOMAN Is it something ¹⁴ _____ them?

HUGO No, ¹⁵ _____ cotton. ¹⁶ _____ to tie your shoes.

WOMAN Oh, you mean shoelaces!

Reading and Writing Portfolio 5 p72

6 Decisions and choices

Language Summary 6, Student's Book p128

6A Make up your mind

make and do

1 Choose the correct word.

1 You are lazy! You've *done*/*made* nothing all weekend!
2 Have you *done/made* a decision yet?
3 I've *done/made* a lot of progress in English since I started.
4 Did you *do/make* a degree?
5 He's *done/made* me lots of favours.
6 Look at the mess you've *done/made*!
7 He often *does/makes* excuses about being late.
8 Have you *done/made* any work today?

2 Replace the phrase in **bold** with the correct form of *do* or *make* and a phrase in the box.

> ~~mistake~~   the washing   me laugh
> a course   the washing-up   up your mind

> *made a mistake*

1 I've **done something wrong** in this exercise.
2 I like him because he**'s funny**.
3 Have you **cleaned the clothes**?
4 I'm **studying** at an evening school at the moment.
5 Do you want more time to **decide**?
6 Would you mind **cleaning the dishes** with your brother?

First conditional

3 Write first conditional sentences.

1 If you / make dinner, I / do / the washing-up.
    If you make dinner, I'll do the washing-up.
2 / you / do / me a favour if I / help / you do your homework?

    ----

3 You / not / pass if you / not do / any work.

    ----

4 What / you / say / if she / not make up / her mind soon?

    ----

5 They / never learn / if they / be allowed to / behave so badly.

Future time clauses

4 Match beginnings 1–8 to endings a)–h).

1 I won't be able to cook dinner until
2 They'll be exhausted tomorrow unless
3 We'll write to you as soon as
4 She'll do a degree unless
5 After we get your letter,
6 When I finish the housework
7 Before she does a degree,
8 As soon as they start making a noise,

a) they go to bed early.
b) she'll have to pass her exams.
c) I might do the shopping.
d) they'll have to go to bed.
e) we make a decision.
f) we'll make a decision.
g) I've done the shopping.
h) she fails her exams.

5 Fill in the gaps with the correct form of these verbs. Use the Present Simple or *will*.

> ~~do~~   make   put   get   release   check

1 I *'ll do* the cleaning when you've tided up this mess.
2 As soon as she _____ her new album, I'll buy it.
3 After I've sorted this stuff out, I _____ everything away.
4 I won't phone him until we _____ into a hotel.
5 Unless he _____ some progress, he won't pass.
6 _____ we _____ there before they do?

6 Read the conversation and choose the correct words.

VIC OK. I'm leaving now.

DAD Where will you stay ¹(when)/if you get there?

VIC At the youth hostel ²if/unless we find a good hotel.

DAD And if the youth hostel is full?

VIC We'll worry about that ³before/when we get there.

DAD Well, ⁴as soon as/until you've left, we'll probably start worrying.

MUM And we'll worry ⁵until/as soon as you ring tomorrow.

VIC I'll only call you ⁶after/unless I find a place to stay.

DAD But don't call ⁷before/after ten. I'm looking forward to having a lie-in tomorrow.

MUM A lie-in? But ⁸unless/if Vic's away, we can decorate his room.

VIC No way! Promise me you won't do anything ⁹until/after I get back.

DAD OK. We won't touch your room ... ¹⁰if/unless you forget to phone us.

7 Rewrite the sentences with *unless*.

1 If the weather isn't bad, we'll meet in the park.

Unless the weather's bad, we'll meet in the park.

2 If you don't tell me about the problem, I won't be able to help. _____

_____

3 If your employees don't have time to relax, they won't work well. _____

_____

4 She should be here later if she doesn't make another excuse! _____

_____

5 We'll have to get a loan if you don't start making more money. _____

_____

6 He'll continue to make the same mistakes if we don't do anything. _____

_____

6B **Protective parents**

Reflexive pronouns

1 Fill in the gaps with a reflexive pronoun.

1 My daughter made the decision _herself_.

2 The washing-up isn't going to do _____ you know!

3 We really enjoyed _____ last night. Thanks very much.

4 My son made dinner for the whole family by _____ last night!

5 Dave and Polly designed their cottage _____.

6 Simon! If you don't like the way I've done it, do it _____!

7 Promise me that you will both look after _____.

8 I didn't need any help – I made up my mind _____.

Zero conditional; conditionals with modal verbs and imperatives; *in case*

2 Fill in the gaps in the conversation with the correct form of these verbs.

| ~~buy~~ go (x 2) book call send get be |

PAT My son's just gone on holiday to Italy with his friends. They didn't book a hotel or anything.

MARY Don't worry. My daughter only ¹ _buys_ a flight when she ² _____ away.

PAT But when we ³ _____ on holiday, we always ⁴ _____ a room in advance!

MARY Yes. And when we ⁵ _____ there, I still ⁶ _____ my parents. Nowadays I ⁷ _____ lucky if my daughter ⁸ _____ me a postcard.

3 **a)** Fill in the gaps in these clauses with *If* or *When*.

1 ....*If*.... you don't like the present,

2 .*When*. I finish an exercise,

3 .... you live to be 100 in the UK,

4 .... I'm older,

5 .... this bus stops,

6 .... he doesn't feel better soon,

7 .... you get up in the morning,

8 .... you finish a meal,

b) Write zero or first conditional sentences. Use the *if/when* clauses in **3a)** and these words.

1 you / not / have to / keep it.

If you don't like the present,

you don't have to keep it.

2 I / check / the answers immediately.

3 you / get / a letter from the Queen.

4 I / start / saving some money.

5 you / help / me with these bags?

6 we / have to / call the doctor.

7 you / listen / to the radio?

8 you / always do the washing-up?

4 Read Lucy's tips and fill in the gaps. Use a modal and the verb in brackets or the imperative of the verb. Sometimes more than one answer is possible.

Lucy Samuel has been helping parents for over 20 years with their teenage children. She shares a few of her tips with us.

- If you want to show your children you love them, ¹ ...*spend*... (spend) time with them. And when you haven't got time, you ² ...*shouldn't make*... (not make) excuses. Explain to them why you're busy.

- If you want your children to talk to you, you ³ _____ (not tell) anyone their secrets. Teenagers need to trust you and if they can't do that, why ⁴ _____ they _____ (tell) you anything?

- Teenagers see everything you do. Unless you can stop doing something yourself, for example smoking, how ⁵ _____ you _____ (expect) your children to stop?

- If you remember anything at all about your younger days, you ⁶ _____ (remember) being a teenager. It's a confusing time. When children come to you for advice, ⁷ _____ (listen). Their problems may be different from those you had.

- Teenagers will argue with you – it's part of growing up. But if you argue with them, ⁸ _____ (not expect) things to get better.

5 Fill in the gaps with *if* or *in case*.

1 I'll read the instructions ...*in case*... they say anything useful.

2 We should make some extra food now _____ he changes his mind.

3 I'm not making him dinner _____ he won't help me with the washing-up.

4 We don't buy travel insurance _____ we aren't going abroad.

5 We always buy travel insurance _____ we have an accident.

6 I ring my brother _____ my car breaks down.

7 Take a mobile phone with you _____ the car breaks down.

8 Read the instructions first _____ you don't want to break it.

6C Touch wood

Reading

1 Read the article and fill in the gaps with these sentences.

a) ~~In fact, many successful people simply got a 'lucky break'~~

b) But the pieces of paper he used kept falling out

c) A young, relatively unknown singer was asked to take over

d) He decided to move the family to Australia

e) A week later she had a part in a film

2 Are these sentences true (T), false (F) or the article doesn't say (DS)?

1 | F | The article says that people become successful because they work hard.

2 | | Aretha Franklin used to sing in her church.

3 | | Sarah Michelle Gellar's acting career started slowly at first.

4 | | Luciano Pavarotti became world-famous in 1963.

5 | | Mel Gibson's parents were millionaires.

6 | | Mel Gibson had a fight at the audition for *Mad Max*.

7 | | Post-It™ notes were invented in 1974.

8 | | Spencer Silver invented Post-It™ notes by himself.

Synonyms V6.3

3 Read the article again and match words 1–6 to synonyms a)–f).

1 break   a) role
2 legendary   b) opportunity
3 part   c) discovery
4 unknown   d) trying
5 invention   e) unheard of
6 attempting   f) very famous

Serendipity

We tend to think that successful people deserve their success. They probably studied hard at school, they worked hard every day or they took a lot of risks. ¹*In fact, many successful people simply got a 'lucky break'* : something happened that gave them a chance to be successful; they took the opportunity and the rest, as they say, is history.

Some people just fell into fame. Aretha Franklin, the legendary Queen of Soul, was singing in her church choir* when a record company executive heard her voice. Sarah Michelle Gellar, star of *Buffy the Vampire Slayer*, was in a restaurant when a TV executive saw her. She was four. ² _____

_____ .

A month later she was in an advert for Burger King.

Other people were lucky because someone else was unlucky. In 1963 the very famous Italian opera singer Giuseppe di Stefano had a throat problem while he was singing in the opera *La Bohème*.

³ _____ .

His name? Luciano Pavarotti.

Some people are just very lucky. Mel Gibson was born in New York. In 1968 his dad won a lot of money on a quiz show.

⁴ _____ .

In Sydney Mel studied drama because his sister sent off his application form. Then the night before one of his first auditions, Mel had a fight at a party. And when the unheard-of actor arrived at the audition, he looked awful – but perfect for the role of Mad Max. He got the part.

Sometimes lucky breaks lead to a new invention. When that happens, it's called serendipity. The discovery of Post-It™ notes were an accident. In 1970 Spencer Silver was attempting to make a strong type of glue. He failed. Then four years later, Spencer's colleague was trying to mark the songs in a hymn book at his local church.

⁵ _____

_____ .

He remembered Spencer's glue and the Post-It™ was born. Last year 3M sold over $100 million worth of the notes.

In life, it seems, sometimes you need a little luck. But while you're waiting, it's probably safer to keep working hard.

*choir = a group of people who sing together in a church, school, etc.

6D **What's your opinion?**

Discussion language RW6.1

1 **You are at a meeting. Choose the best response for each situation.**

1 You are speaking and someone interrupts you.
a) Be quiet!
b) Can I just finish what I was saying?
c) Sorry, do you mind if I interrupt?

2 Someone is speaking. You want to say something.
a) Can I make a point here?
b) If I could just finish making this point.
c) What's the point of this?

3 You know Jason has an opinion, but he hasn't said anything yet.
a) That may be true, but what about Paul?
b) Jason, you had something you wanted to say.
c) Sorry, do you mind if Paul interrupts?

4 Someone is speaking and you have the same opinion as him/her.
a) Yes, I'd agree with that.
b) Sure, go ahead.
c) I'm sure I agree, actually.

2 **Complete the conversations with these phrases.**

> ~~What's your opinion~~   Go ahead   Can I just
> That may be   You had something   I'm not sure
> Yes, I'd agree with   Can I just finish

1

TIM   ¹ _What's your opinion_ of teenage behaviour?

ANN   It's simple. Firstly, parents should be stricter.

TIM   ² _____ that. But the reasons ...

ANN   ³ _____ what I was saying?

TIM   Sure. ⁴ _____ .

2

PAM   ⁵ _____ you wanted to say about superstitions.

CARL   Yes, statistics show that Friday 13ᵗʰ isn't unluckier than any other day.

PAM   ⁶ _____ true, but the worst days for accidents last year were all Fridays.

AL   ⁷ _____ say something here?

⁸ _____ about Fridays in general, but the idea that Friday 13ᵗʰ is actually an 'unlucky day' is ridiculous.

> of course   I agree actually   make a point here
> That's not   If I could just finish   What do you think
> Yes, sure   I interrupt

3

KIM   Can I ⁹ _____ ?

MEL   Yes, ¹⁰ _____ .

KIM   Mel, you must agree that tourism is good for the country.

MEL   ¹¹ _____ .

KIM   And that we need more hotels.

MEL   I'm not sure ¹² _____ .

4

JAN   ¹³ _____ about prefabs?

ELLA   I hate them. They're ugly and poor quality ...

JAN   Sorry, do you mind if ¹⁴ _____ ?

¹⁵ _____ true actually. In Sweden ...

ELLA   ¹⁶ _____ making this point.

JAN   Yes, sorry. Go ahead.

Review: gradable and strong adjectives

3 **Change the words in bold to make these sentences more positive. Use *absolutely* and an adjective in the box.**

> ~~fascinated~~   delighted   fantastic   furious
> tiny   gorgeous   delicious   filthy

1 I was **quite interested**. _absolutely fascinated_

2 The room was **quite small**. _____

3 The weather was **good**. _____

4 His house was **fairly dirty**. _____

5 My husband was **angry**. _____

6 The food was **quite tasty**. _____

7 She looks **beautiful**. _____

8 We were **very pleased**. _____

 Reading and Writing Portfolio 6 p74

REAL WORLD • REAL WORLD • REAL WORLD • REAL WORLD • REAL WORLD • REAL WORLD • REAL WORLD

7 Technology

Language Summary 7, Student's Book p130

7A Save, copy, delete

Computers (1) and (2) V7.1 V7.2

1 Find seven more pieces of computer equipment in the puzzle (→, ↓ or ↘).

M	C	M	P	R	I	N	T	E	S	S
P	E	S	C	A	N	N	E	R	S	P
K	R	M	C	A	M	S	C	A	C	E
E	R	I	O	R	S	O	E	U	A	A
Y	S	E	N	R	O	R	U	E	N	K
B	C	R	M	T	Y	O	I	S	N	E
O	R	U	O	I	E	S	S	R	E	R
B	E	S	U	E	E	R	T	P	A	S
K	E	Y	B	O	A	R	D	I	O	Y
O	S	S	C	R	E	E	N	E	C	O
M	O	N	I	T	O	R	I	S	D	K

2 Cross out the incorrect words.

1 save *a document/an email/a hard disk*

2 delete *a document/a link/a folder*

3 make a back-up copy of your *icons/hard disk/documents*

4 print *an email/a folder/a document*

5 log on to *the Internet/online/ your computer*

6 click on *an icon/a website address/ a password*

Ability G7.1

3 **a)** Read the advertisement for a computing course and choose the correct words.

http://www.surfdirect.co.uk/courses/

Surf direct

In the 21st century, you ¹can't/couldn't ignore computers or the Internet. They're a necessary part of life and they ²can/are brilliant at save you time and money. This two-day course is suitable for beginners who have used a computer, but find email and the Internet difficult ³understand/to understand. You should have some experience of computers and ⁴can/be able to use a mouse and a keyboard. And if you haven't got a clue how ⁵start/to start, then don't worry! Click here for details of our basic computing course.

At the end of our **Surf direct** course, you will:

- know how ⁶to set up/setting up an email account, and read and send emails.
- ⁷can/be able to search the Internet accurately.
- ⁸could/be able to buy something on the Internet safely.

b) Read about the experiences of three people who went on the course. Fill in the gaps with the correct form of the verb in brackets (infinitive, infinitive with *to* or verb+*ing*).

I can't ¹ _____thank_____ (thank) you enough for this course. I hadn't got a clue how ² _____ (use) email before I did **Surf direct**. If I ever managed ³ _____ (send) anything, I'd always ring the person to check it had arrived! **Robert, Newcastle**

We're addicted! We're still useless at ⁴ _____ (send) emails, but we're brilliant at ⁵ _____ (search) the Internet for the lowest prices. My husband was able to ⁶ _____ (find) a book I wanted for half the price it is in the shops. Unfortunately we also managed ⁷ _____ (order) two copies, but never mind! Great course. Thanks. **Pat, Sunderland**

My children use the Internet for their homework every night. I was always hopeless at ⁸ _____ (help) them and I hadn't found anyone who could ⁹ _____ (help) me. Now I'm better at ¹⁰ _____ (understand) search results than they are. And I find the Internet easy ¹¹ _____ (use). Of course, I still have no idea how ¹² _____ (work) the video recorder! **Diane, Sheffield**

35

4 Rewrite these sentences using the words in brackets.

1 My daughter can use a computer much better than me. (know how)

   My daughter knows how to use a computer much

   better than me.

2 I never remember passwords. (hopeless at)

   ....

3 My parents don't have a clue how to get broadband. (no idea)

   ....

4 I was able to send an email, but I don't know if it arrived. (manage)

   ....

5 I could get emails, but I couldn't send any. (be able to; not be able to)

   ....

Review: verb patterns

5 Complete sentence b) so it has the same meaning as sentence a).

1 a) She doesn't let her sister borrow her clothes.

   b) She doesn't allow *her sister to borrow her clothes.*

2 a) I'd rather stay at home.

   b) I'd prefer ....

3 a) He continues to phone me every night.

   b) He keeps ....

4 a) They said to me, "Buy a house with a garden."

   b) They told ....

5 a) It looked like it was closed.

   b) It seemed ....

7B Want it, need it!

Electrical equipment V7.3

1 Look at the pictures. Write the names of the electrical equipment needed.

hand-held computer ....

Second conditional G7.2

2 Choose the correct words.

1 She *did/would* check her email more often if she *had/has* broadband.

2 If it *wouldn't/didn't* cost so much, *I'll/I'd* get one tomorrow.

3 We *spent/would spend* less time on the Internet if there *was/were* more things to do.

4 If they *saved/are saved* their documents more regularly, they *lost/wouldn't lose* them.

5 You *didn't/wouldn't* have this problem if you *made/make* back-up copies of your hard disk.

6 *Do/Would* you get air conditioning if you *would be able to/could* afford it?

7 If he *weren't/wouldn't be* so arrogant, more people *would ask/will ask* for his advice.

8 If I *give/gave* you a hand-held computer, *do/would* you use it?

3 Complete sentence b) so it has the same meaning as sentence a).

1 a) I might do a computer course. Then I'd use the computer more.

b) I'd use the computer more if <u>I did a computer course.</u>

2 a) Our central heating doesn't work and I'm freezing.

b) If our heating _____ , I wouldn't feel so cold.

3 a) We don't have a GPS and we're lost!

b) We _____ if we had a GPS.

4 a) He can't record it on DVD. He doesn't have a DVD recorder.

b) If he had a DVD recorder, he _____ record it on DVD.

5 a) I can't remember my password so I can't use my computer.

b) If I _____ my password, I could use my computer.

6 a) I have no idea how to do this or I would help you.

b) I would help you if I _____ how to do this.

First conditional **G6.1** Second conditional **G7.2**

4 Choose the correct ending for each sentence.

1 Will you lend me yours if ...
a) I promise to look after it?
b) I promised to look after it?

2 If it cost about half as much, ...
a) we'll be able to buy one.
b) we'd be able to buy one.

3 The program will start automatically if ...
a) you click on the document icon.
b) you clicked on the document icon.

4 If I were you, ...
a) I'll get an MP3 player.
b) I'd get an MP3 player.

5 If you forget your password, ...
a) we'll send you a reminder.
b) we'd send you a reminder.

6 Would it be more comfortable if ...
a) it has air conditioning?
b) it had air conditioning?

5 a) Read about a competition and fill in the gaps with the correct form of the verbs in brackets.

What You Want competition

These people answered the question: If you ¹ <u>could</u> (can) buy any piece of electronic equipment, what ² <u>would</u> it <u>be</u> (be)?

Read the descriptions and guess the answers! If you ³ <u>answer</u> (answer) all four questions correctly, you ⁴ <u>'ll have</u> (have) a chance of winning this month's What You Want competition.

a) It ⁵ _____ (be) absolutely freezing when I ⁶ _____ (get) home. This house was built over 200 years ago and it simply didn't exist then.

b) If I ⁷ _____ (not do) it tonight, I ⁸ _____ (find) it all in the kitchen tomorrow morning. If we ⁹ _____ (get) one, we ¹⁰ _____ (have) a lot more time in the evenings and we definitely ¹¹ _____ (not argue) so much!

c) I go jogging a lot and the one that I have is useless and I keep having to change the CDs. If I ¹² _____ (have) one of these, the music wouldn't finish all the time and I ¹³ _____ (be able to) carry a lot more music.

d) You aren't allowed to use mobiles in the car without one now. The trouble is I spend a lot of time driving. If I ¹⁴ _____ (not speak) to people, I won't get anything done. Anyway, I'll just have to buy one. If I ¹⁵ _____ (not do) it soon, I ¹⁶ _____ (get) a fine.

b) What is each person talking about in 5a)? Write the names of the electrical equipment.

a) <u>central heating</u>
b) _____
c) _____
d) _____

37

7C Virus alert!

VOCABULARY AND READING

Reading

1 Read the article and write questions a)–e) in the correct places 1–5.

a) ~~What is spyware?~~
b) How do I get rid of it?
c) What can it do?
d) How does it get on to my computer?
e) Is spyware a common problem?

Spyware

Nobody likes a computer virus, but at least you can get rid of it. And there is a lot of anti-virus software these days. It can find a virus, fix it and you can forget about it. Unfortunately the same isn't true for spyware.

1 _What is spyware?_
Spyware is software that hides somewhere on your computer. It collects information about what you do on the Internet and passes this information to companies without your permission. If you shop on the Internet and use your credit card, you should know that some spyware can record this information!

2 _____
Your computer can catch spyware in lots of ways. If you open the wrong email, or even visit the wrong website, spyware can download itself onto your computer. And spyware often comes with free software.

3 _____
Most spyware just collects information about your surfing habits for advertising reasons. But some spyware can be more powerful and will often make your computer slower. Adware is a type of spyware which is advertising software. It makes 'pop-up' advertisements appear while you are connected to the Internet. Not dangerous ... but very annoying.

4 _____
If this is the first time you've heard of spyware, you've probably got some on your PC. Surveys have found that 90% of computers have several pieces of spyware on them. And spyware will stay on your computer for a long time, quietly collecting information and sending it back to its authors.

5 _____
There is some anti-spyware software that will remove most of your problems. However, some anti-spyware software is spyware itself, so be careful! For a complete list of software, go to spywarewarrior.com.

2 Read the article again and answer these questions.

1 Why can it be difficult to find spyware?
Because it hides on your computer.

2 Why is spyware important if you buy things online?
_____

3 Can you get spyware if you're not using the Internet?
_____

4 What kind of information can spyware collect?
_____

5 Why does most spyware want this information?
_____

6 How might you know your computer has spyware on it?
_____

7 What percentage of computers are not infected with spyware?
_____

8 What advice is given about removing spyware?
_____

Use of articles: a, an, the, no article `V7.4`

3 Read these comments on the article and fill in the gaps with *a, an, the* or – (no article).

Frankie
There are now laws against spyware in [1] _the_ USA. Criminals behind [2] _____ most serious software can be sent to [3] _____ prison for five years and get [4] _____ fines of over [5] _____ million dollars!

Rory
Thanks for [6] _____ article. I get 'pop-up' advertisements all [7] _____ time and I had no [8] _____ idea that there was [9] _____ reason for them all. I'll visit [10] _____ site.

Tess
[11] _____ expert in [12] _____ California estimates that spyware writers are making up to $2 billion dollars [13] _____ year. [14] _____ fine for writing this annoying stuff should be [15] _____ higher!

What's the password?

Indirect and direct questions

Indirect and direct questions RW7.1

 1 Which question in each pair is more polite? Choose a), b) or both if you think they are both polite.

1 a) What's the time, please?
  b) Do you know what the time is?

2 a) Can you tell me what happened?
  b) Have you any idea what happened?

3 a) Do you think you could send it to me?
  b) Please could you send it to me?

4 a) Is he coming later?
  b) Do you know whether he is coming later?

5 a) Could you tell me what the password is?
  b) What's the password?

2 Match beginnings 1–6 to endings a)–f) in these indirect questions.

1 Do you know whether broadband
2 Have you any idea whether
3 Could you tell
4 Do you know
5 Can you tell me if there
6 Do you think he

a) will be able to help me?
b) is a password for this?
c) how this scanner works?
d) he's made a back-up?
e) is available here?
f) me how I save a document?

 3 Correct the mistakes in the phrases in **bold** in these indirect questions.

a webcam is

1 Do you know **what ~~is a webcam~~**?

2 Could you tell me **how do I download software**?

3 Can you tell them **what are the passwords**?

4 Do you know how much **does air conditioning cost**?

5 **Do you think if we can** log on without a password?

6 Have you any idea **where could I buy** a GPS?

4 Rewrite direct questions 1–8 in the conversations using the phrases in brackets.

1

JACK   Hi. I'm Jack. I need to use this PC. ¹What's Sean's password? (Can you tell me) *Can you tell me what Sean's password is?*

ISABELLA   Sorry, I don't know.

JACK   ²Is he at home today? (Do you know) ....

ISABELLA   Yes, he is. He isn't well.

JACK   ³What's his phone number? (Have you any idea) ....

ISABELLA   No, I'm sorry. I'll ask the secretary.

2

JACK   Sean, it's Jack Ross from accounts. I need to use your PC. ⁴Can I get your password? (Could you tell me) ....

SEAN   Er ... ⁵Could you use another PC? (Do you think) ....

JACK   Sorry. There aren't any.

SEAN   ⁶Is there a girl with dark hair opposite you? (Can you tell me) ....

JACK   Yes, long dark hair.

SEAN   Er ... OK. My password is I–S–A B–E–L–L–A. It's er ... a place in Italy.

JACK   Very interesting. Isa Bella. I've never heard of it.

SEAN   ⁷Could you speak more quietly, please? (Do you think) ....

JACK   Are you OK, Sean?

 Reading and Writing Portfolio 7 p76

8A Changing weather

Weather V8.1

1 Correct the **bold** words/phrases.

1 A tornado is a type of **snow**. *wind*

2 A shower is a **long** period of rain.

3 **Lightning** makes a noise.

4 When it's humid, the air is **dry**.

5 A gale is a type of **rain**.

6 A gale is **more** violent than a hurricane.

7 Fog makes it difficult to **hear** things.

8 A heat wave is a period of **cool** weather.

9 Floods happen where there is too **little** water.

2 Cross out four letters from each word and label the thermometer.

1 b̶r̶o̶y̶i̶l̶l̶i̶n̶g̶s̶
2 tchielliey
3 kcewooll
4 vwoawrmn
5 hauoght
6 frieaezzinng

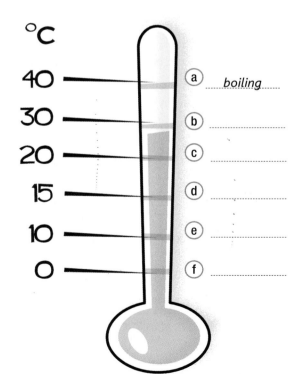

°C

40 — a *boiling*

30 — b _____

20 — c _____

15 — d _____

10 — e _____

0 — f _____

The passive G8.1

3 Choose the correct active or passive verb form.

1 The UK *gets*/*is got* some of its gas from the North Sea.

2 Several agreements *have made*/*have been made* to try and reduce greenhouse gases.

3 The full environmental effects won't *understand*/*be understood* for many years.

4 Wear something warm – I heard the weather will *change*/*be changed* later.

5 Thousands of people *kill*/*are killed* every year in storms and hurricanes.

6 Climate change *is affecting*/*is being affected* the weather all over the world.

7 It *felt*/*was felt* a lot chillier yesterday.

8 Many simple things can *do*/*be done* to prevent climate change.

4 Read sentences 1–4. Then choose sentence a) or b) to continue.

1 I recycle as much rubbish as possible.
   a) I use three rubbish bins for different materials.
   b) Three rubbish bins are used by me for different materials.

2 My car is environmentally friendly.
   a) Someone designed it to use petrol and electricity.
   b) It was designed to use petrol and electricity.

3 Deserts are getting larger.
   a) They can only be stopped by planting new trees.
   b) People can stop them by planting new trees.

4 We use over 18 billion tins and cans every year in the UK.
   a) We recycle about 4 billion of them.
   b) About 4 billion are recycled by us.

5 Fill in the gaps with the passive form of the verbs. Use the Present Simple, Past Simple, Present Perfect Simple or *will*.

The hurricane season in 2005 was one of the worst on record. Two of the worst hurricanes [1] _*were reported*_ (report) in North America: Hurricanes Katrina and Rita.

Since 1953, Atlantic hurricanes [2] _____ (give) names from lists written by the National Hurricane Centre. Only women's names [3] _____ (use) at first, but in 1979 men's names [4] _____ (add). Now there are six lists of names and hurricanes [5] _____ (name) in alphabetical order from the lists. So the list that [6] _____ (use) in 2004 [7] _____ (not use) again until 2010. For example, the first hurricane of 2004 was Hurricane Alex. And the first hurricane in 2010 [8] _____ (call) Hurricane Alex. The names of serious hurricanes [9] _____ (not repeat). For example, in 2005, Katrina and Rita [10] _____ (remove) from the list. Since 1954, 62 names [11] _____ (retire) from the list.

 8B Recycle your rubbish

Containers V8.2

 1 Which container can we use for each group of things? Use the containers in the box.

| bottle | tin | box | can |
| bag | jar | packet | carton |

1 _*a bottle of*_ milk, orange juice, wine
2 _____ sweets, chips [US], shopping
3 _____ tuna, beans, cat food
4 _____ tissues, chocolates
5 _____ cola, lemonade, beer
6 _____ orange juice, milk, soup
7 _____ coffee, marmalade, honey
8 _____ tissues, crisps, sweets

 2 Read the shopping list. Tick the usual containers. Correct the unusual containers.

Shopping

1 *a ~~can~~* _bottle_ *of olive oil*
2 *a box* _✓_ *of washing powder*
3 *a box* _____ *of potatoes*
4 *a tube* _____ *of soup*
5 *a packet* _____ *of biscuits*
6 *a tin* _____ *of honey*
7 *a carton* _____ *of milk*
8 *a bag* _____ *of butter*

Quantifiers G8.2

3 Look at the picture and complete the sentences. Use *There's/There are* and *not any*, *not much*, *not many* or *a lot of*.

1 _There isn't much_ food.
2 _____ boxes.
3 _____ paper.
4 _____ tins.
5 _____ rubbish.
6 _____ bottles.
7 _____ jars.
8 _____ bread.
9 _____ cans.
10 _____ cartons.

4 Fill in the gaps with *a few* or *a little*.

1 I've got __a few__ chocolates.
2 The weather is _____ warm today, isn't it?
3 Would you like _____ more coffee?
4 There are _____ empty bottles for recycling.
5 Could you buy _____ tins of cat food?
6 I'll give you _____ help if you wait _____ minutes.
7 He knows _____ words of French and he speaks _____ English.

5 Rewrite the sentences using the words/phrases in brackets. Make other changes if necessary.

1 There's a bit of soup in the fridge. (much)
   There isn't much soup in the fridge.

2 We've got more than enough time to get there. (plenty)
   _____

3 Hardly any people I know recycle plastic. (few)
   Only _____

4 I'm a little too tired to go out tonight. (bit)
   _____

5 Oliver hasn't got many teeth, but he's only six months old. (hardly)
   _____
   _____

6 A lot of children recycle things at school. (loads)
   _____

7 There's hardly any olive oil in the cupboard. (only a little)
   _____

8 There isn't any time left. (no)
   _____

6 Choose the correct words.

ROSE Adam. If you've got [1]*a few/* (*enough*) time, can you put the recycling bin out?

ADAM There's [2]hardly *any/much* rubbish in it.

ROSE That's strange. Adam! Look in the other bin! [3]*Much/Lots of* this stuff can be recycled.

ADAM But there isn't [4]*any/no* paper in there. I checked.

ROSE What about glass? There are [5]*a lot/loads of* bottles in here.

ADAM Sorry. You're right. Actually, I can see [6]*a little/a few* tins too.

ROSE And there's more than [7]*a little/a few* plastic.

ADAM Plastic? Can [8]*much/many* plastic be recycled?

ROSE Yes, I think so. You know, [9]*a bit of/hardly any* care could save our planet.

ADAM I know. Sorry. Look, there's [10]*a few/hardly any* room in the recycling bin now.

ROSE Stop making excuses! There's [11]*plenty/several* of room.

8C Dangers at sea

Word formation (2): prefixes and opposites,
other prefixes and suffixes **V8.3** **V8.4**

1 **a)** Read the first part of the article. Fill in gaps 1–6 with the correct word, a), b) or c).

1 a) (sleepless)   b) oversleep   c) sleepy
2 a) unaccurate   b) disaccurate   c) inaccurate
3 a) unfair   b) underfair   c) fairless
4 a) harmful   b) harmless   c) unharmful
5 a) replay   b) implay   c) playful
6 a) incommon   b) uncommon   c) overcommon

The Orca

If you think you have a ¹ _sleepless_ baby, consider this: baby killer whales don't sleep for the first month of their life so their mothers have to stay awake too!

In fact, the name 'killer whale' is a little
² _____ and also ³ _____ .
Firstly, killer whales (or orcas) are not really whales. They're in fact the largest member of the dolphin family. Secondly, they are usually ⁴ _____ to humans. There are no records of any orca attacks on humans in the wild.

Instead, these animals are highly sociable and even quite ⁵ _____ They live in groups called 'pods', with between 5 and 30 orcas, for their whole lives. And it is very ⁶ _____ to see one swimming alone.

b) Read the second part of the article and add the correct suffix or prefix to words 7–16. Use these suffixes and prefixes.

> Suffixes: -ful, -less
> Prefixes: re-, im-, under-, over-, ir -, dis-, un- (x 2)

The orcas' friendly and cooperative nature is very ⁷use _ful_ for finding food. Orcas hunt in their pods and then work together to kill. In 1999 a BBC team filmed a pod hunting a grey whale and its calf. The journalist described the event:

"The desperate calf* was fighting for its life and I wanted the orcas to finish their job quickly. But the mother was ⁸tire_____ in her attempts to protect her calf. Her job was an ⁹_____possible one."

The total worldwide population of orcas is ¹⁰_____known, but is thought to be around 100,000. It is likely that we have ¹¹_____estimated how many there are because they live in all of the world's oceans. Although they haven't been hunted since 1981, scientists believe their numbers are decreasing. In particular, ¹²_____fishing and oil accidents are reducing their food supplies.

There are about 40 orcas in aquariums all over the world, but many people ¹³_____agree with keeping them in these conditions and believe it's ¹⁴_____responsible. The most famous orca, Keiko, who appeared in the 1993 film *Free Willy*, was in an aquarium until scientists attempted to ¹⁵_____introduce him into a pod in the wild. The $20 million attempt was ¹⁶_____successful, however, and Keiko swam 1,400 kilometres on his own to Norway where he spent the last two years of his life.

*calf = a young whale

2 Read both parts of the article again. Are these sentences true (T), false (F) or the article doesn't say (DS)?

1 [T] Killer whales are not a type of whale.

2 [ ] A human has never been killed by an orca.

3 [ ] Orcas hunt alone.

4 [ ] In the description, the young grey whale survives.

5 [ ] There are probably more than 100,000 orcas in the world.

6 [ ] In 1981 hunting whales was made illegal.

7 [ ] Pollution is a problem for orcas.

8 [ ] Keiko was found in an aquarium in Mexico.

9 [ ] Keiko became part of a pod when he was released.

Warnings and advice RW8.1

1 **a) Make sentences with these words.**

a) think / should / we / visit / do you / Which ?

Which do you think we should visit?

b) the streets / you / Make sure / the stadium / around / avoid .

c) careful / in / Vine Street / you're / Be / when .

d) heard / hadn't / before / that / I .

e) you / advice / give / Could / some / me ?

f) I wouldn't / were you / I / him / listen to / if .

g) make the / same mistake / or else you'll / in summer / Don't go / as I did .

h) really / thanks / That's / useful .

b) Complete the conversation with sentences a)–d) from 1a).

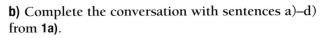

JON   We're looking for a house in your area, Clare. Here's some information about a few places.

        ¹ *Which do you think we should visit?*

CLARE   Hmm. ² _____

        It's a bit of a bad neighbourhood.

JON   Vine Street? ³ _____

        Thanks. Anything else?

CLARE   ⁴ _____

JON   The football stadium? Is it noisy?

CLARE   Yes, it can be.

c) Complete the conversation with sentences e)–h) from 1a).

NINA   Mike, you've been to the Caribbean, haven't you?
        ⁵ _____

        When is it a good time to go?

LIZ   ⁶ _____

        He spent his Caribbean holiday in his hotel room!

MIKE   That was because it was the start of their hurricane season. ⁷ _____

        _____

        My holiday was a disaster, so I <u>would</u> listen to my advice!

NINA   ⁸ _____

        I had no idea. So you went in the summer?

MIKE   Yes, in August.

Review: indirect and direct questions

2 **Rewrite these direct questions as indirect questions. Use the words/phrases in brackets.**

1 Did you reply to his email? (Could you tell)

   Could you tell me if you replied to his email?

2 Is Argentina hot at this time of year? (Do you know)

   _____

   _____

3 Who sells maps around here? (Can you tell)

   _____

   _____

4 Should I book a hotel before I go? (Do you think)

   _____

5 Why is it so expensive? (Have you any idea)

   _____

 Reading and Writing Portfolio 8 p78

Answer Key

1A Be happy!

1a) 2 the house 3 to people online
4 relatives

b) 2 tidy up the house 3 chat to people online 4 visit relatives

2 b) Have you been clubbing in the last month? c) When are you next having a quiet night in? d) How often do you have people round for dinner?
e) Have you ever chatted to people online? f) Did you have a lie-in last weekend? g) Are you visiting friends or relatives this weekend? h) How many exhibitions did you go to last year?

3 2 When are you next having a quiet night in? 3 Did you have a lie-in last weekend? 4 Have you ever chatted to people online? 5 Have you been clubbing in the last month?

4a) 2 – 3 did 4 do 5 do 6 is 7 has 8 –

b) 2 Andy (always cooks). 3 When she was a teenager. 4 Every Friday.
5 Because they've got two young children. 6 Because it's her best friend's birthday. 7 None. 8 Megan (did).

1B Love it or hate it

1a) 2a) 3b) 4f) 5g) 6i) 7h) 8c) 9d)

b) A2; 6; 9 B3 C4; 5; 7; 8

2 2a) says 3c) have used 4c) were
5a) have 6c) try 7c) 'm not making
8c) 's

3 2 was 3 didn't use 4 wrote 5 haven't been able to 6 call 7 don't get
8 'm helping

4 2 no one 3 Neither of them
4 usually 5 always 6 All of 7 I think

5 2 He doesn't think the computer's got a virus. 3 I didn't understand anything he said. 4 We always used our computer to do serious things.
5 There are lots of computers at my school. 6 Joe hasn't repaired my laptop. 7 All of my colleagues can type quickly. 8 Both of our parents can use computers. 9 He works with computers all day so he needs one at home. 10 We are using the latest software.

6 2 **I go** swimming … 3 Who **works** with … 4 … have you **been** to?

5 … I **walked** to … 6 **I think** you are correct. 7 **I play** a lot …
8 **I've lived** in … 9 **I went** to …
10 Who **do** they work with?/Who does **he/she** work with?

1C The best medicine

1 2 embarrassed 3 nervous 4 relaxed
5 disappointed 6 confused 7 glad
8 stressed

2a) 2 at 3 on 4 in 5 with 6 by

b) 2T 3F 4F 5DS 6T 7F

1D At a barbecue

1a) 2 don't 3 doesn't 4 hasn't 5 haven't
6 didn't 7 isn't 8 haven't

b) b) It isn't going to rain c) They haven't got any children d) We didn't see him yesterday e) He hasn't been here before f) You haven't told him yet g) Clare doesn't eat beef h) I don't need to bring anything to the barbecue

2 2 aren't you 3 don't they 4 didn't they 5 isn't he 6 isn't it 7 haven't I
8 haven't we?

3 3 We're going home soon, aren't we?
4 You haven't met our neighbours, have you? 5 You didn't drive here, did you? 6 It's warm outside, isn't it?
7 He wants something to eat, doesn't he? 8 You don't know Sam, do you?
9 He's got the address, hasn't he?
10 You've tried English sausages, haven't you? 11 He isn't working this weekend, is he? 12 I'm not late, am I?

4 2 Everyone **wants** to … 3 **They're** going to … 4 I often **lose** against …
5 He's worked here **since** the …
6 I've **been** to … 7 … Paul and **Sally's** dog. 8 Nobody **wants** to …

2A Slow down!

1 2g) 3b) 4d) 5h) 6f) 7j) 8c) 9i)
10e)

2 2 have to 3 allowed 4 ought
5 should 6 allowed 7 supposed
8 Can 9 're allowed to 10 be able to
11 must 12 ought

3 2 You ought to take a week off.
3 I'm not able to meet you tonight.

4 You aren't/You're not allowed to work at weekends. 5 You don't have to wear a tie. 6 You must arrive before 9 a.m. 7 The company is supposed to give us holiday pay.
8 You mustn't leave work before 4 p.m.

4a) 2 How are you able to work long hours when you have a family?
3 Should we be under a lot of pressure at work? 4 Ought we to tell him that he's becoming a workaholic? 5 Are you allowed to wear informal clothes at your work?
6 Do we have to take time off in the summer? 7 Are we supposed to take all our holiday before December?

b) b)6 c)3 d)5 e)4 f)2 g)7

2B Ready, steady, eat

1 a) broccoli b) fridge c) grill d) peas
e) freezer f) aubergine g) beef
h) frying pan i) courgette
j) microwave k) lamb l) red pepper
m) oven n) toaster o) cooker
p) blender q) rubbish bin r) wok
s) carrots t) saucepan

```
S O P O B R O C C O L I O
A E R E D P E P P E R C A
U L T E P F R E E Z E R U
C O V E N S F R I D G E B
E R U B B I S H B I N C E
P R B L E N D E R G B O R
A R C O O K E R P R A U G
N C A R R O T S E I R R I
R E B E E F U B A L G N
T O A S T E R U S L E E N
O F R Y I N G P A N J T E
B M I C R O W A V E U T G
B W O K I L A M B P E E K
```

2 2 fry 3 roast; bake 4 heat up;
microwave 5 boil; steam 6 grill

3a) 2 'm heating up 3 aren't helping
4 are … making 5 'm working;
'm not eating 6 is growing

b) 8 Does he know I'm here? 9 The Spanish and Italians cook more than the British. 10 Over 60 million people live in the UK. 11 He doesn't work on Fridays. 12 I don't think so.

c) a)4 b)1; 5 c)3; 6 d)11 e)9; 10 f)8; 12

4a) 2 'm sitting 3 're doing 4 is
5 always takes 6 don't think
7 Do you remember 8 are still trying

Answer Key

b) 2 'm writing 3 's cooking 4 doesn't understand 5 use 6 's doing 7 says 8 're trying 9 Do … eat 10 tastes

2C It's a nightmare

1 2 haven't had nightmares 3 didn't sleep a wink 4 dozes off 5 having a lie-in 6 get back to sleep 7 's fast asleep 8 is a light sleeper

2 1c) 2b) 3a)

3 2 Because our eyes move quickly in different directions. 3 Because our body becomes more relaxed. 4 We dream and we cannot move at all. 5 Because scientists think that REM sleep is important for memory and learning. 6 Giraffes, adults, babies, bats.

4 3 really/incredibly/extremely 4 really/incredibly/extremely 5 really/absolutely 6 really/absolutely 7 really/incredibly/extremely 8 really/incredibly/extremely 9 really/absolutely 10 really/absolutely

2D What's the matter?

1 2c) 3b) 4b) 5a)

2 2e) 3d) 4b) 5a)

3 2 Why don't you 3 I've tried that 4 Yes, I see what you mean 5 Have you tried 6 Well, it's worth a try 7 I'm sorry to hear that 8 I'd take 9 that's a good idea 10 I can see why you're upset 11 You ought to 12 might try that

3A Your holiday, my job

1 2 setting off 3 see you off 4 've checked into 5 put up with 6 get around 7 get back 8 pick me up

2 2 Have … worked 3 've … brought 4 've … got back 5 haven't checked into 6 've … dealt

3 2 ✓ 3 We've run a bed and breakfast **for** three years. 4 I like your house. How long **have you lived** here? 5 Mark isn't here. **He's gone** to work. 6 **We set off** hours ago, but we're stuck in traffic. 7 ✓ 8 **Have you checked** into the hotel yet? 9 ✓

4 2 've always loved 3 didn't take 4 've worked 5 joined 6 've been 7 've never felt 8 's learned 9 haven't cooked 10 've dealt with 11 couldn't 12 have … eaten 13 've drunk 14 've roasted 15 has complained

3B Lonely Planet

1a) 2 go on 3 get

b) b) on your own c) a journey/a cruise d) a cruise/a journey e) a taxi to work/out of a car f) out of a car/a taxi to work

2 2 Marta has been giving guided tours since she was 16. 3 I've been looking forward to my holiday for six months. 4 Cambridge University Press has been publishing books since 1584. 5 We've been going out together since I was 18. 6 You've been living in this house for two months.

3 2 been travelling 3 stayed 4 been feeling 5 tried 6 had 7 been looking after 8 kept/been keeping 9 published 10 had 11 finished 12 explored/been exploring

4 3 How many hotels have you worked in? 4 How many times have you been on a package holiday? 5 How long has he been taking work home? 6 How many times have you got a taxi to work? 7 How long have you been studying English? 8 How long have Tony and Maureen been married?

5 2 have … been getting around 3 haven't been 4 's been shining 5 've been going 6 hasn't taken 7 Have … known 8 haven't travelled 9 's been standing

3C Call that a holiday?

1 2 danger 3 enormous 4 important 5 sadness 6 serious 7 fame 8 modesty 9 accident

2 2c) 3a) 4b) 5c) 6b)

3 2 dangerous 3 enormous 4 important 5 sadness 6 serious 7 famous 8 modesty 9 accident

3D A trip to India

1 1 of 2 with; with 3 about/by; with 4 about; with

2a) 2 Is there anything worth seeing here? 3 Have you got any other tips? 4 What about places near the sea? 5 What's the best place to hire a car?

b) 2 What's the best place to hire a car? 3 Is there anything worth seeing here? 4 What about places near the sea? 5 Have you got any other tips?

3 2 'd recommend 3 sounds wonderful 4 's the best 5 wouldn't go

6 really useful 7 Do you know any 8 bother 9 to know 10 And is there 11 should go to 12 And what about 13 It's probably best 14 Have you got any 15 You really must 16 I've heard

4A Riders

1 2 appear 3 seeing 4 go 5 Going 6 playing 7 have

2 2 went 3 threw 4 was holding 5 were finishing 6 had 7 was 8 was wearing 9 wore 10 were playing 11 was 12 died 13 lost 14 was 15 was singing 16 hit 17 fell 18 was staying 19 asked 20 wanted 21 wasn't joking 22 painted

3 2 was; used to wash 3 used to be; preferred 4 lost; was; used to earn 5 used to present 6 didn't use to be; changed; did … use to be

4B Adventures

1 2b) 3a) 4c) 5b) 6c) 7c) 8a)

2 2 'd sold out 3 hadn't driven 4 hadn't heard 5 had left 6 hadn't done 7 'd been 8 hadn't known

3a) 2 stayed 3 got back 4 hadn't tidied up 5 was 6 had arranged 7 hadn't set 8 had arrived 9 was

b) b); d); e)

4a) 2 weren't 3 'd been 4 got back 5 'd lost 6 got 7 had found 8 saw 9 had got 10 had had to

b) 2d) 3f) 4b) 5c) 6e)

5 3 has 4 would 5 is 6 had 7 would 8 is; has 9 would; had 10 –; has

4C Natural medicines

1 c)

2a) 2 verb 3 verb 4 verb 5 noun 6 adjective 7 verb 8 adjective

b) 2a) 3b) 4a) 5b) 6a) 7a) 8b)

3 2DS 3T 4F 5F 6F 7F 8T

4D It's just a game!

1 2 bad-tempered 3 violent 4 rude 5 arrogant 6 offensive 7 spoilt 8 loyal 9 lazy 10 loud

2 2c) 3b) 4e) 5a)

3 2 He tends to be 3 On the whole 4 Generally speaking 5 violent 6 a bit arrogant 7 impolite 8 aggressive

4 2 They aren't very considerate at times. 3 Some of them can be rather untidy. 4 They tend to be a bit better with money. 5 Generally speaking, most women like shopping. 6 On the whole, they tend to be more organised than men.

5A Moving house

1 2 The Stephens Family 3 James and Mel 4 Sam

2 2 loft 3 study 4 kitchen 5 bathroom 6 garage 7 cellar
↓ cottage

3 2B 3B 4P 5H 6P 7B 8B

4 2 as close 3 similar 4 much less 5 far 6 the least 7 little 8 best 9 most

5 2 favourite 3 interesting 4 cheaper 5 most character 6 most determined 7 better 8 lightest 9 busiest 10 more fashionable 11 further

5B A load of old junk

1 2 sorted 3 Put 4 throwing 5 go 6 give 7 throw 8 coming 9 tidied 10 take

2a) 2e) 3a) 4d) 5c)

b) 2b) 3a) 4d) 5e)

3 2 'll 3 will 4 're going to 5 're looking 6 'll sort it out 7 'm going to work

4 2 What **are you** going to do with all those old clothes? 3 I'm **playing** cards so I'll be back late. 4 Yes, it's going **to** be a big change. 5 I'll **call** you this evening about the meeting. 6 **I'll tidy** it up before they come back.

5 2 Are … going to buy 3 'll find 4 'll be 5 'll need 6 I'm … not going to listen 7 Will … give/Are … going to give 8 I'll sell 9 will buy 10 'll tidy 11 'm not doing 12 'll help 13 'm meeting 14 'll give 15 'm taking 16 are … going to tidy/will … tidy 17 'll do

5C Flatpack world

1 b)3 c)5 d)4 e)2

2 2 The minimum number of flats in each BoKlok community. 3 The year BoKlok began selling housing. 4 The number of homes BoKlok has sold. 5 The countries where prefabs were popular after World War II.

3 2 Prefabs seem to be more popular nowadays. 3 Over 2,000 people in Scandinavia have decided to buy a BoKlok home. 4 In the future more people might live in prefabs. 5 Many people would like to buy their own home. 6 I don't mind living with my parents.

5D Is this what you mean?

1 2 glass 3 leather 4 cotton 5 cardboard 6 plastic 7 metal 8 wool 9 wood 10 paper

2a) 2a) 3d) 4e) 5c) 6f)

b) 2c) 3a) 4d) 5b) 6f)

3 2 Do you mean 3 what they're called 4 They're usually 5 It's stuff for 6 the word for 7 it's made of 8 You mean 10 It's a type of 11 you're looking for 12 What's it called 13 I'm looking for 14 for cleaning 15 they're made of 16 You use them

6A Make up your mind

1 2 made 3 made 4 do 5 done 6 made 7 makes 8 done

2 2 makes me laugh 3 done the washing 4 doing a course 5 make up your mind 6 doing the washing-up

3 2 Will you do me a favour if I help you do your homework? 3 You won't pass if you don't do any work. 4 What will you say if she doesn't make up her mind soon? 5 They'll never learn if they're allowed to behave so badly.

4 2a) 3e) 4h) 5f) 6c) 7b) 8d)

5 2 releases 3 'll put 4 check 5 makes 6 Will … get

6 2 unless 3 when 4 as soon as 5 until 6 after 7 before 8 if 9 until 10 unless

7 2 Unless you tell me about the problem, I won't be able to help. 3 Unless your employees have time to relax, they won't work well. 4 She should be here later unless she makes another excuse! 5 We'll have to get a loan unless you start making more money. 6 He'll continue to make the same mistakes unless we do something.

6B Protective parents

1 2 itself 3 ourselves 4 himself 5 themselves 6 yourself 7 yourselves 8 myself

2 2 goes 3 go 4 book 5 get 6 call 7 'm 8 sends

3a) 3 If 4 When 5 When 6 If 7 When 8 When

b) 2 When I finish an exercise, I check the answers immediately. 3 If you live to be 100 in the UK, you get a letter from the Queen. 4 When I'm older, I'll start saving some money. 5 When this bus stops, will you help me with these bags? 6 If he doesn't feel better soon, we'll have to call the doctor. 7 When you get up in the morning, do you listen to the radio? 8 When you finish a meal, do you always do the washing-up?

4 3 shouldn't tell 4 should; tell 5 can; expect 6 must remember 7 listen 8 don't expect

5 2 in case 3 if 4 if 5 in case 6 if 7 in case 8 if

6C Touch wood

1 2e) 3c) 4d) 5b)

2 2T 3F 4DS 5DS 6F 7T 8F

3 2f) 3a) 4e) 5c) 6d)

6D What's your opinion?

1 2a) 3b) 4a)

2 2 Yes, I'd agree with 3 Can I just finish 4 Go ahead 5 You had something 6 That may be 7 Can I just 8 I'm not sure 9 make a point here 10 of course 11 Yes, sure 12 I agree actually 13 What do you think 14 I interrupt 15 That's not 16 If I could just finish

3 2 absolutely tiny 3 absolutely fantastic 4 absolutely filthy 5 absolutely furious 6 absolutely delicious 7 absolutely gorgeous 8 absolutely delighted

7A Save, copy, delete

1

Answer Key

2 2 a link 3 icons 4 a folder 5 online 6 a password

3a) 2 can 3 to understand 4 be able 5 to start 6 to set up 7 be able to 8 be able to

b) 2 to use 3 to send 4 sending 5 searching 6 find 7 to order 8 helping 9 help 10 understanding 11 to use 12 to work

4 2 I'm hopeless at remembering passwords. 3 My parents have no idea how to get broadband. 4 I managed to send an email, but I don't know if it arrived. 5 I was able to get emails, but I wasn't able to send any.

5 2 I'd prefer to stay at home. 3 He keeps phoning me every night. 4 They told me "Buy a house with a garden." 5 It seemed to be closed.

7B Want it, need it!

1 b) GPS/sat nav c) dishwasher d) washing machine e) hair dryer f) hair straighteners g) hands-free phone h) air conditioning i) central heating j) MP3 player k) DVD recorder l) webcam

2 2 didn't; 'd 3 would spend; were 4 saved; wouldn't lose 5 wouldn't; made 6 Would; could 7 weren't; would ask 8 gave; would

3 2 worked 3 wouldn't be lost 4 would be able to 5 could remember 6 had any idea

4 2b) 3a) 4b) 5a) 6b)

5a) 5 's/is 6 get 7 don't do 8 'll find 9 got 10 'd/would have 11 wouldn't argue 12 had 13 'd/would be able 14 don't speak 15 don't do 16 'll/will get

b) b) dishwasher c) MP3 player d) hands-free phone

7C Virus alert!

1 2d) 3c) 4e) 5b)

2 2 It can record your credit card information. 3 Yes, it often comes with free software. 4 Information about your surfing habits. 5 For advertising reasons. 6 Your computer is slower or you are getting a lot of 'pop-up' advertisements. 7 10%. 8 Use some anti-spyware software or visit spywarewarrior.com.

3 2 the 3 – 4 – 5 a 6 the 7 the 8 – 9 a 10 the 11 An 12 – 13 a 14 The 15 –

7D What's the password?

1 2b) 3a) 4a) and b) 5a)

2 2d) 3f) 4c) 5b) 6a)

3 2 how I download software 3 what the passwords are 4 air conditioning costs 5 Do you think we can 6 where I could buy

4 2 Do you know if he's at home today? 3 Have you any idea what his phone number is? 4 Could you tell me your password? 5 Do you think you could use another PC? 6 Can you tell me if there's a girl with dark hair opposite you? 7 Do you think you could speak more quietly, please?

8A Changing weather

1 2 short 3 Thunder 4 wet 5 wind 6 less 7 see 8 hot 9 much

2 b)5 hot c)4 warm d)3 cool e)2 chilly f)6 freezing

3 2 have been made 3 be understood 4 change 5 are killed 6 is affecting 7 felt 8 be done

4 2b) 3a) 4a)

5 2 have been given 3 were used 4 were added 5 are named 6 was used 7 won't/will not be used 8 will be called 9 aren't/are not repeated 10 were removed 11 have been retired

8B Recycle your rubbish

1 2 a bag of 3 a tin of 4 a box of 5 a can of 6 a carton of 7 a jar of 8 a packet of

2 3 bag 4 packet/tin/carton 5 ✓ 6 jar 7 ✓ 8 packet

3 2 There aren't any boxes. 3 There's a lot of paper. 4 There aren't many tins. 5 There's a lot of rubbish. 6 There are a lot of bottles. 7 There aren't many jars. 8 There isn't much bread. 9 There aren't any cans. 10 There are a lot of cartons.

4 2 a little 3 a little 4 a few 5 a few 6 a little; a few 7 a few; a little

5 2 We've got plenty of time to get there. 3 Only a few people I know recycle plastic. 4 I'm a bit too tired to go out tonight. 5 Oliver has got hardly any teeth, but he's only six months old. 6 Loads of children recycle things at school. 7 There's only a little olive oil in the cupboard. 8 There's no time left.

6 2 any 3 Lots of 4 any 5 loads of 6 a few 7 a little 8 much 9 a bit of 10 hardly any 11 plenty

8C Dangers at sea

1a) 2c) 3a) 4b) 5c) 6b)

b) 8 tire**less** 9 **im**possible 10 **un**known 11 **under**estimated 12 **over**fishing 13 **dis**agree 14 **ir**responsible 15 **re**introduce 16 **un**successful

2 2T 3DS 4F 5T 6DS 7T 8DS 9F

8D Be careful!

1a) b) Make sure you avoid the streets around the stadium. c) Be careful when you're in Vine Street. d) I hadn't heard that before. e) Could you give me some advice? f) I wouldn't listen to him if I were you. g) Don't go in summer or else you'll make the same mistake as I did. h) That's really useful thanks.

b) 2 Be careful when you're in Vine Street. 3 I hadn't heard that before. 4 Make sure you avoid the streets around the stadium.

c) 5 Could you give me some advice? 6 I wouldn't listen to him if I were you. 7 Don't go in the summer or else you'll make the same mistake as I did. 8 That's really useful thanks.

2 2 Do you know if Argentina is hot at this time of year? 3 Can you tell me who sells maps around here? 4 Do you think I should book a hotel before I go? 5 Have you any idea why it's so expensive?

9A Get healthy!

1 2 operating 3 doctor 4 A&E 5 specialist 6 GP 7 ward 8 attack 9 asthma 10 migraine 11 allergy 12 prescription 13 chemist's

2 2 whose 3 where 4 who/that 5 whose 6 when 7 which/that 8 who/that 9 where

3 2a) 3e) 4h) 5c) 6g) 7i) 8f) 9j) 10d)

4a) 3O 4S 5O 6O 7S 8O

b) 3 (The people the allergy affects ...); 5 (The patient the surgeon operated on ...); 6 (The ward I stayed in ...); 8 (The migraines he gets ...)

5 2 I'm going on a retreat I think you've been on. 3 She's the woman who/that runs an organic fruit and vegetable shop. 4 I think it's very interesting you decided to become a surgeon. 5 I regularly get migraines which/that are really painful. 6 He's got a disease I'd never heard of.

9B Good news, bad news

1 **News story A**
2e) 3b) 4g) 5d) 6h) 7c) 8f)
News story B
2e) 3g) 4c) 5f) 6d) 7h) 8b)

2 2 I've just been **offered** another job. 3 **Have you** just changed the TV channel? 4 Her new record still hasn't **been** released. 5 The prime minister hasn't said **anything yet**. 6 Scientists **have already** discovered some causes of migraines. 7 Have you **been** paid for that survey yet? 8 You **still haven't** told anyone.

3 2 The reports haven't been published yet. 3 I've never taken part in a demonstration. 4 The offer has just been rejected by the government. 5 The unions have already called off the strike. 6 The government hasn't met last year's targets yet. 7 Four surveys have been carried out so far. 8 Have they already taken him to hospital?

4 2 If I were you, I'd get bottled water. 3 You'd better see a dentist soon. 4 Is it a good idea to book ahead? 5 Whatever you do, don't feed the animals. 6 Don't leave any valuables in your car.

5 3 hasn't been seen 4 has been 5 has … published 6 have shocked 7 have … been charged 8 has been released 9 haven't given 10 has suffered 11 has been 12 has been seen 13 has been finished 14 has … been released 15 has … received

9C Faking it

1 1 Ed Devlin 2 Maximillian Devereaux 3 Jatinder Sumal

2 2 Cutting up onions. 3 He thinks his body language at football matches wasn't good enough. 4 Her friends said it was a really good show. 5 At a film premiere. 6 She couldn't think of anything to ask him. 7 She doesn't plan to leave her job.

3 2 Despite not managing to persuade the experts, he enjoyed the experience. 3 She had never heard of *Faking It*. However, her friends said it was a really good show. 4 She tried to interview Robbie Williams. However, she couldn't think of anything to ask him! 5 Although it was a terrible experience, Jatinder quickly recovered. 6 In spite of her success at 'faking it', Jatinder doesn't plan to leave her job.

9D At the doctor's

1 1 runny; sneeze 2 poisoning, sick; diarrhoea 3 Paracetamol; painkiller; pill 4 symptom; asthma; wheezy 5 infection; antibiotics; virus

2 2d) 3e) 4c) 5b) 6f)

3a) b) getting c) taking d) suffering e) getting f) a week g) take them h) some antibiotics i) another appointment j) a prescription

b) 2b) 3d) 4c) 5e)

c) 6j) 7h) 8g) 9i) 10f)

10A The anniversary

1 2 lost 3 got in 4 gave 5 left 6 called 7 kept in 8 get 9 from 10 'm 11 know

2 2T 3F 4T 5T

3 2b) 3b) 4a) and b) 5a) and b)

4a) 2d) 3f) 4h) 5b) 6a) 7e) 8g)

b) 2 The room wasn't supposed to be big, but … 3 I was going to have a party that weekend, but … 4 I was supposed to invite him, but … 5 The concert was supposed to end at nine, but … 6 No one was going to give them anything, but … 7 We were going to meet in the morning, but … 8 I was supposed to get in touch with Diana, but …

10B Who's that?

1a) 1 … he's **going** bald. 2 He's got **short dark** hair and **a** striped shirt. 3 She's got straight blonde **hair** and a **flowery dress**. 4 She's got **shoulder-length** hair and a light jacket.

b) a) Erin b) Alice c) Chris d) Oscar

2 1b) Jay's hair is shoulder-length and wavy. c) Fern's hair is long and curly. 2a) Alice has got light trousers. b) Chris has got a plain jacket. Oscar has got a striped jacket.

3a) 2 The girl with the ponytail could be Ruby. 3 Jo could be stuck in traffic. 4 Joel might be coming to the party later. 5 Stephen must be leaving in a minute. 6 The children may prefer to stay at home. 7 The weather can't get any worse. 8 Simon can't be working there any more.

b) 2F 3T 4T 5T 6F 7T 8F

4a) 2 must 3 may 4 could 5 can't 6 must 7 might 8 must 9 can't

b) 3 Phoebe must be having a baby soon. 4 Leo could/may/might be Phoebe's grandfather. 5 Chris can't be staying at the party until late. 6 Phoebe and Leo must get on well. 7 Erin and Maisie could/may/might be chatting about Oscar. 8 Jay can't be retired yet.

10C The party's over

1 2c) 3e) 4a) 5b)

2 b) pointed out c) going up d) get out of it e) put it off f) split up g) looked up h) came across i) get over it j) had come up with

3 2F 3F 4T 5F 6F 7T 8F

10D Do you mind?

1 2b) 3a) 4b)

2 1 No, do whatever you like. 2 May/Can; Yes, help yourself. 3 Is it OK if; Of course./I'm afraid I'm watching this. 4 Would you mind if; I'd rather he didn't. 5 Could/May; I'd rather you didn't./Yes, sure. 6 Do you think; Yes, of course.

3a) 2 Do you think I could have a glass? 3 Is it OK if I make some coffee? 4 Can I look round your garden? 5 Would you mind if I checked my email? 6 Do you mind if I have a shower?

b) 2 Yes, of course you can 3 Yes, of course it is 4 Go ahead 5 Sorry, you can't 6 No, not at all

Answer Key

11A Any messages?

1 2 sorts 3 was 4 organised 5 working 6 did 7 spend 8 going 9 get

2 2 problems 3 deadlines 4 shifts 5 overtime 6 responsible 7 department

3 2b) 3b) 4f) 5e) 6d) 7a)

4 2 sorted out as many problems as she did 3 she had been in charge of the company for a month last May 4 she had organised two conferences by herself 5 she couldn't stand working shifts any more 6 she had done a lot of unpaid overtime last month 7 she had to spend more time with her family 8 she was going for an audition next week for an acting job 9 she would be in touch after the audition

5 2 told her he didn't have to work tonight so he was going to pick up the children from school. 3 told him the dentist wasn't well today so he had to call to rearrange his appointment. 4 She told them she would be at home this afternoon if they wanted to ring her.

11B How did it go?

1 1 challenging 2 badly-paid 3 dull 4 well-paid 5 stressful 6 temporary 7 repetitive 8 permanent 10 rewarding 11 part-time 12 full-time

2a) 2b) 3g) 4j) 5e) 6h) 7c) 8f) 9a) 10d)

b) 2 if I 3 would; didn't get 4 had looked 5 my last job was

c) 7 They asked me if anyone in my family lived in the UK. 8 They asked me how many people I knew in Edinburgh. 9 They asked me if I would email them my referee's phone number. 10 They asked me how long I was planning to stay in the UK.

3 2 She told Carlos to use plenty of vocabulary. 3 She told Carlos not to get nervous. 4 He told Carlos to speak clearly. 5 He told Carlos to listen to the questions carefully. 6 He told Carlos not to be late. 7 He asked Carlos if he could check the time of his exam. 8 He asked Carlos if he could tell him the questions later.

11C Undercover

1 b)

2 2 him to give out 3 him to improve 4 to tell Nkem 5 giving tickets 6 to cancel parking tickets 7 to stealing credit cards 8 to investigate the problem 9 to believe the problem

3 1 Because drivers sometimes threaten to hurt PAs. 2 Because he is an undercover reporter. 3 Because he wasn't giving out enough tickets. 4 Stolen credit cards. 5 They refused to believe the problem was serious.

11D It's my first day

1a) 2d) 3b) 4e) 5f) 6c)

b) Ask someone to repeat information: 2; 5 Check information: 3; 4; 6

2 2i) 3d) 4h) 5c) 6f) 7e) 8g) 9b) 10j)

3 2 give it to 3 say that 4 is that 5 tell me 6 I didn't 7 are you talking 8 do you mean 9 what did you say 10 is that 11 is your

12A I wish!

1a) 2 I'm not really into clubs. 3 I reckon there's a simple solution. 4 I'm sick of having no money. 5 I don't feel up to it tonight. 6 I'm broke until the end of the month.

b) b)2 I'm not really into clubs. c)5 I don't feel up to it tonight. d)6 I'm broke until the end of the month. e)4 I'm sick of having no money. f)3 I reckon there's a simple solution.

2 2 I can't be bothered to do the washing-up tonight. 3 Are you off? 4 Why are you hanging around? 5 I want to have a go at starting my own website. 6 I could do with a shower.

3 2 didn't rain 3 could 4 was/were 5 were staying 6 were doing

4a) 2 I could go 3 they weren't wearing jeans and trainers 4 I knew how to drive 5 I didn't have to leave early 6 I wasn't/weren't so tired

b) b) wouldn't; were able to c) could; would be able to d) Would; could e) were; would look f) would meet; didn't

c) 2d) 3e) 4b) 5c) 6f)

12B Important moments

1a) 2h) 3b) 4d) 5f) 6a) 7i) 8c) 9e)

b) a)8; 9 b)3; 4; 7 c)1; 2; 6

2 2 get in touch with 3 got into trouble 4 got here 5 getting around/to get around 6 got the job 7 getting older 8 getting rid of

3a) 2 would have; got 3 hadn't; wouldn't have 4 wouldn't have; 'd 5 hadn't; wouldn't have 6 wouldn't have; hadn't

b) 1b) Yes. 2a) No. b) No. 3a) No. b) Yes. 4a) No. b) Yes. 5a) Yes. b) Yes. 6a) Yes. b) Yes.

4 2 would … have met; hadn't been 3 had got; 'd have got 4 wouldn't have seen; hadn't bought 5 hadn't encouraged; wouldn't have become 6 wouldn't have been; had let 7 hadn't got; 'd have had 8 'd have left; had failed

5a) 2 got 3 had 4 split up 5 went 6 felt 7 took 8 started 9 got 10 asked

b) 2 would have; hadn't had 3 hadn't felt; wouldn't have gone out 4 had gone; would have been 5 wouldn't have taken; been 6 hadn't been; wouldn't have 7 wouldn't have asked; hadn't got on 8 hadn't given

12C Superheroes

1 2D 3A 4B 5E

2 2 entertaining 3 embarrassed 4 preferred 5 created 6 predictable 7 creativity 8 confused 9 successful 10 successful 11 acting

3 2F 3F 4DS 5T 6DS 7F 8F 9DS

Reading and Writing Portfolio 1

1 a) Anna's mum. b) Anna, David, Eve and Harry. c) She's on holiday.

2 2b) 3b) 4a) 5b) 6c)

3b) 2 article 3 pronoun and auxiliary verb 4 preposition 5 pronoun 6 pronoun

c) b)6 c)3 d)2 e)5 f)4

4 2 In 3 I; the 4 I; have 5 Have; you 6 We; have 7 It; is 8 We; are

Reading and Writing Portfolio 2

1 a)E b)B c)C d)F e)D

2 2T 3T 4T 5F 6DS

3b) 2 n/s 3 vgc 4 ono 5 p/w 6 eves. 7 Tue. 8 Tel. no.

c) 2 Avenue 3 April 4 for example 5 as soon as possible 6 including 7 Road 8 Thanks

4 **Possible answers**
a) 3 hours p/w on Sat. morning.
Call Alex
Tel. no. 01923 434325
(after 7 eves.)
b) Double room to let
£140 p/w incl. bills
n/s only
mjparks@ukmail.net
c) Television for sale
2 months old – vgc
£120 ono
Pick up only from Carston Ave.
Call Tom
Tel. no. 07986 304207

Reading and Writing Portfolio 3

1a) 2T 3T 4F You should start a new paragraph for each new subject. 5F You should use full forms. 6T

b) 2

2 2b) 3a) 4b) 5c) 6b) 7a)

3a) 1 UK 2 US 3 UK

b) 2 03/14/07 3 apologize 4 color 5 traveler 6 through

4a) 2 You should start a new paragraph for each new subject. 3 You should use full forms. 4 You should write your signature above your name.

b) Possible answers
21/12/06 → 12/21/06
realise → realize
14th March (14/03/07) → March 14th (03/14/07)
Yours sincerely → Sincerely (yours)

Reading and Writing Portfolio 4

1 b)

2 2c) 3a) 4b) 5b) 6c)

3 b)2 c)1 d)3

4 2b); d) 3a)

5 2a) 3b) 4f) 5d) 6c)

6 2 attracted 3 'm … learning 4 takes 5 describes 6 is 7 is 8 are 9 'll love 10 'm going to read

7 2 The book tells the story of a young boy who has no parents. 3 The main character in the book is Jack. 4 The story takes place in Buenos Aires, Argentina. 5 I think the book would make a good film because it's so exciting. 6 The title of the book is *Loyal* because it refers to the relationship between the man and his dog.

Reading and Writing Portfolio 5

1 2c) 3a) 4b) 5b) 6a) 7a) 8c)

2 2F 3F 4T 5T 6T 7F

3a) 2 We're so sorry that we didn't come to Jackie and Bill's party on Saturday afternoon. 3 Don't forget to book train or plane tickets soon if you're going to come! 4 Can anyone tell me what Pat Austin's email is? 5 Hope you all have a lovely break during the holiday! 6 We're so grateful for all your cards and presents. 7 What happened was that we were supposed to finish packing in the afternoon. 8 Would you all like to come?

b) b)3 c)5 d)6 e)8 f)1 g)7 h)4

c) a)1 b)3; 8

4a) 2 Hope you have 3 Can anyone tell me 4 We'd rather 5 We are so grateful for 6 Would you like 7 What happened was that 8 Don't forget

b) Possible answers
2 **Don't forget** that it's Mum and Dad's wedding anniversary tomorrow.
3 **Can anyone tell me** where the station is, please?
4 **I'm so grateful for** my birthday present. **Hope you have** a good time on holiday.
5 **Would you like** to come to a pop concert on Friday? **I'd rather** go with someone than go alone.

5a) 1c) 2a) 3b)

Reading and Writing Portfolio 6

1 a) Barry b) Phil c) Nicole

2 2T 3F 4DS 5T 6T 7F 8F 9DS

3a) 2 I've always felt that … 3 I have no doubt that … 4 As far as I'm concerned, … 5 As I see it, … 6 I'm positive that … 7 To me, … 8 I strongly believe that …

b) 3; 6; 8

c) 2 **As far as he's concerned**, we pay less than the government's minimum wage! 3 **As they see it**, they have to earn their pocket money. 4 **We strongly believe that** this is a much better idea than the threat of no pocket money.

4a) 2 She's absolutely convinced that she will win. 3 I've always felt that everyone should be able to afford a house. 4 He has no doubt that we will find life on other planets. 5 I'm positive that I saw him earlier. 6 As she sees it, housework is a waste of time. 7 To me, children spend too much time watching TV. 8 As far as my brother is concerned, children shouldn't get pocket money.

Reading and Writing Portfolio 7

1 2D 3B 4A

2 2T 3F 4T 5DS 6T 7F 8F

3 3; 4; 7

4a) Then; Next; Meanwhile; Finally

b) 1 next 2 finally 3 meanwhile 4 first

5a) 2 **Don't forget** to switch the machine off when it's finished! 3 **Remember that** the rubbish is collected early on Monday mornings. 4 **You will need** to put the bins outside on Sunday night. 5 **Whatever you do**, don't use the sink in the upstairs bathroom. 6 **Try to avoid** using too much heat otherwise you will burn the onions.

b) a)4 b)6 c)5 d)1; 3

6a) 3; 4; 7

b) Possible answers
2 Check the channel for Big Brother. (I think it's Channel Four.) 3 Change the channel on the DVD recorder. 4 Press the red record button.

7 1 need to/will need to 2 Make sure 3 Remember that 4 Avoid using 5 Don't forget to 6 Whatever you do

Answer Key

Reading and Writing Portfolio 8

1a) Letter 1: A; C Letter 2: B; F; D

b) a)1 b)2

2 2T 3T 4F 5T 6DS 7T 8F 9DS

3 1F 2C; D; 3B; E

4a) 1 Furthermore; Moreover
2 Although; However; even though

b) 1 even though 2 however 3 in addition; furthermore; moreover

5a) C For example, students should **be told** ...; ... three or four bins, that **are emptied** regularly, ... D ... the park should **be closed** ... F When I am not worrying about hitting a pedestrian or **being attacked** ...; Nothing **has been done** about this ...

b) 1; 3

6 2 Even though 3 Furthermore
4 Even though/Although 5 Moreover
6 In addition/Furthermore
7 However

7 2 The road must be repaired
3 Recycling bins aren't used regularly.
4 The bins are never emptied. 5 A lot of glass is recycled 6 I was told that the lights would be replaced.

Reading and Writing Portfolio 9

1 c); d); f); h)

2 2 Yes, she does. 3 Developing training programmes, giving advice and training to instructors.
4 To develop her skills in a full-time position with more responsibility and work as part of a team. 5 She ran in this year's London Marathon.
6 Her CV. 7 Probably hard-working, organised and quite ambitious.

3 2B 3E 4A 5C

4a) b)1 c)4 d)3 e)6 f)2

b) 1 to; in; for 2 At; as 3 from; to
4 in; for 5 As; from 6 to; from

5a) A; C; E; B

b) I am writing **in** reply to your advertisement **in** The Times **for** a receptionist at St John's Wood Surgery.

At the moment I am working full-time **as** a receptionist for a large American bank in London. My responsibilities range **from** meeting visitors to answering phones and taking messages.

I am interested **in** medical issues and three years ago, I had a temporary position **as** a secretary **at** the Wellington Hospital. I believe my experience, interest and enthusiasm would be excellent for your position.

As you will see **from** my CV, I have over nine years of experience. In this time, I have learned a wide variety of skills connected with my work. I have also realised that I particularly enjoy the personal contact that receptionists have with people. Therefore I would like the opportunity to work in a smaller office environment.

I look forward to hearing **from** you.

Reading and Writing Portfolio 10

1 2; 3; 4

2 1 At an old school friend's wedding.
2 Because Fiona liked Kate's shoes.
3 Bright clothes. 4 Kate is tanned and looks Spanish or Italian. She has long, dark hair, is very tall and looks like a model. Fiona looks English, she has short, blonde hair, isn't very tall and doesn't look like a model.
5 Kate is much more confident but she is more disorganised than Fiona.
6 She's always ready with a cup of tea and some good advice when Fiona has a problem.

3 b)3 c)1 d)2

4a) 2 ... **we look** completely different ... **I look** typically English! 3 In fact, **she looks like a** model and ...
4 ... **she's** ... **the** most considerate and unselfish **person I know**.

b) a)3 b)4 c)2

5a) 2b) look intelligent 3b) similar taste in 4b) looks like 5b) the most talented 6b) similar taste in 7b) like my 8b) 's the worst

b) 2 My brother and I have similar taste **in** cars. 3 People think I look ~~like~~ Swedish ... 4 My dad is one of the **funniest** people I know. 5 He looks **like** his father, doesn't he? 6 She looks **good** in that dress.

Reading and Writing Portfolio 11

1 2d) 3g) 4b) 5h) 6c)
Extra events: e); f)

2 2a) 3c) 4b) 5a)

3a) 2 Past Simple: When Jamie **walked** into the offices ... 3 Past Continuous: ... he **was feeling** absolutely terrified.
4 Past Perfect: He'**d** never **been** in such ... 5 Present Simple: **Are** you here for an interview? 6 Present Continuous: **Are** you **feeling** nervous?

b) We usually use **present** verb forms in direct speech in stories.
We usually use **past** verb forms in stories when we describe things that happened.

c) Past Simple; Past Continuous; Past Perfect

4a) 2 had ... met 3 were walking
4 smiled 5 knocked 6 were talking
7 Are ... feeling 8 was 9 had heard
10 couldn't

b) Because the woman he had talked to was his interviewer.

Reading and Writing Portfolio 12

1 a) Steven's letter b) Mia's letter

2 2DS 3T 4T 5F 6F 7T 8DS

3 b)S c)B d)M e)S

4a) 2h) 3b) 4f) 5c) 6g) 7e) 8d)

b) b)1 c)8 d)7 e)3 f)4 g)6 h)2

5 **Description 1**
1 Everyone **says** ... 2 And **they're** right! 3 But every day I **think** how lucky I am to be a father. 4 And I can't believe that I didn't **make** this decision years ago.
Description 2
1 Then, I lay in bed, thinking **about** my life. 2 But while I **was making** it, I ... 3 Two weeks' holiday for **me** and a friend ... 4 If I **hadn't** had it, I wouldn't have made ...

9 Look after yourself

Language Summary 9, Student's Book p134

9A Get healthy!

Health V9.1

1 Fill in the gaps in the vocabulary notebook with these words.

> ~~surgeon~~ GP doctor operating specialist
> A&E asthma prescription ward attack
> allergy migraine chemist's

Relative clauses with *who, that, which, whose, where* and *when* G9.1

2 Fill in the gaps with *which*, *that*, *who*, *whose*, *where* or *when*. Sometimes more than one answer is possible.

1 He eats a lot of stuff __which/that__ is really unhealthy.

2 She's the woman _____ juice diet I tried.

3 After the accident they took her to the A&E department _____ she works.

4 Do you know anyone _____ suffers from migraines?

5 There was a guy on my ward _____ operation was cancelled.

6 Is there a good time _____ I can come and visit you in hospital?

7 There are over 20 hospitals _____ carry out major surgery in London.

8 I know several people _____ don't eat meat, but eat fish.

9 The ward _____ I got the infection was really dirty.

3 Match beginnings of sentences 1–10 to endings a)–j).

1 I think it's a good idea
2 A migraine is a painful headache
3 It's important
4 He gave me some juice
5 It's likely his
6 The headaches
7 A surgery is
8 A fast is a period
9 The juice I tried
10 He's the type of person

a) which sometimes affects your sight, too.
b) you see your GP soon.
c) diet is very unhealthy.
d) whose diet is very unhealthy.
e) you don't eat anything before the operation.
f) when you don't eat food.
g) I get sometimes affect my sight, too.
h) that tasted like dirty water.
i) where you see your GP.
j) tasted like dirty water.

Health

doctors	place of work
1 __surgeon__	in an 2 _____ theatre
hospital 3 _____	in a hospital department, for example 4 _____
5 _____	in a hospital department
6 _____	in a surgery

people

other	
nurse	on a 7 _____

illness	serious	
	have	cancer
		a heart 8 _____
	not serious	

	an infection 9 _____
have	a headache/a 10 _____
	an 11 _____ to something

Doctors give you a 12 _____ and you collect your medicine, tablets, etc. from the 13 _____ .

4 a) Is *who*, *that* or *which* the subject (S) or the object (O) of the relative clause?

1 The GP who Mike has seen ... ___O___

2 A hospital that doesn't have an A&E department ... ___S___

3 The people that the allergy affects ... _____

4 The specialist that is going to speak to you ... _____

5 The patient who the surgeon operated on ... _____

6 The ward which I stayed in ... _____

7 An operation which lasted eight hours ... _____

8 The migraines that he gets ... _____

b) In which phrases in **4a)** can we leave out *who*, *that* or *which*?

___1___ (The GP Mike has seen ...), _____ , _____ ,
_____ , _____

5 Join the sentences. Use *which*, *that*, *who*, *whose*, *where* or *when* if necessary. Make any other changes you need to.

1 I'm on a diet. It doesn't allow me to eat bread or pasta.

I'm on a diet which doesn't allow me to eat bread or pasta.

2 I'm going on a retreat. I think you've been on it.

_____

3 She's the woman. She runs an organic fruit and vegetable shop.

_____

4 I think it's very interesting. You decided to become a surgeon.

_____

5 I regularly get migraines. They're really painful.

_____

6 He's got a disease. I had never heard of it.

_____

9B Good news, bad news

News collocations V9.2

1 Put the news stories in the correct order.

A

a) Paris, France. French surgeons refused to call off   ___1___

b) offer of a shorter working week. They are protesting   _____

c) illness that requires an operation, union leaders   _____

d) in a demonstration next Monday. If someone is taken   _____

e) their strike yesterday and rejected the government's   _____

f) promised that there would be no shortage of surgeons.   _____

g) against long hours and over 2,000 surgeons will take part   _____

h) to hospital in an emergency or is suffering from an   _____

B

a) London, England. A government report that was   ___1___

b) a target of employing 20% more nurses by 2010.   _____

c) the offer of a job in the private sector if they made   _____

d) carried out in ten hospitals all over the UK. These   _____

e) published yesterday has discovered something   _____

f) the same money. The report comes from a survey   _____

g) worrying about nurses. Over 25% would accept   _____

h) results are a problem for a government trying to meet   _____

Present Perfect Simple active and passive for recent events G9.2

2 Correct the mistakes in these sentences.

> has
1 Anyone injured ~~have~~ already been taken to hospital.

2 I've just been offer another job.

3 You have just changed the TV channel?

4 Her new record still hasn't released.

5 The prime minister hasn't said yet anything.

6 Scientists already have discovered some causes of migraines.

7 Have you being paid for that survey yet?

8 You haven't still told anyone.

3 Make sentences with these words.

1 strike again / have / Underground drivers / on / gone .
   Underground drivers have gone on strike again.

2 been / The reports / yet / published / haven't .
   ....
   ....

3 in / part / never / I've / a demonstration / taken .
   ....
   ....

4 has / been / The offer / just / government / by the / rejected .
   ....
   ....

5 already / called / have / off the / The unions / strike .
   ....
   ....

6 last year's / government / The / yet / met / hasn't / targets .
   ....
   ....

7 been / Four / have / so far / surveys / carried / out .
   ....
   ....

8 him / already / they / Have / to hospital / taken ?
   ....
   ....
   ....

4 Rewrite the sentences using the words in brackets.

1 I believe you should take plenty of water. (good idea)
   It's a good idea to take plenty of water.

2 My advice is to get bottled water. (were)
   If ....

3 I advise you to see a dentist soon. (had better)
   ....

4 Is booking ahead sensible? (good idea)
   Is .... ?

5 The worst thing to do is feed the animals. (Whatever)
   ....

6 You should take all your valuables out of your car. (Don't)
   ....

5 Fill in the gaps in these news stories with the verbs in the boxes. Use the Present Perfect Simple active or passive.

| ~~not find~~   ~~have~~   not see |

A missing teenager from West London [1] _has_ still _not been found_ and police say they [2] _have had_ little information about where he could be. Damian Urwin [3] .... since last Tuesday when he left his friend's house in Notting Hill.

| shock   be   publish |

Cleanliness in hospital wards [4] .... in the news recently. The government [5] .... just .... a report about it and the results [6] .... many people.

| charge   not give   release |

Two men [7] .... just .... with the murder of a local businessmen. A third suspect [8] .... from Paddington police station, but police [9] .... the names of the arrested men yet.

| suffer   see   go |

Lucy [10] .... from severe asthma for four years. She [11] .... to several hospitals and [12] .... by some of the best specialists.

| receive   finish   release |

It [13] .... for over a year, but Tom Cruise's new film [14] .... only just .... at cinemas in London and it [15] .... already .... excellent reviews.

Faking it

Reading

 Read the article quickly and write the correct names.

1 Who learned to cook professionally? ....

2 Whose experience involved a sport? ....

3 Who learned how to interview famous people? ....

2 **Read the article again and answer the questions.**

1 Which people successfully 'faked it'?

 Ed Devlin and Jatinder Sumal successfully 'faked it'.

2 What skill does Ed think he has improved?

 ....

3 What did Maximillian think he did wrong?

 ....

 ....

4 Why did Jatinder decide to go on the programme?

 ....

5 Where did Jatinder meet Robbie Williams?

 ....

6 What happened?

 ....

7 What has Jatinder decided to do after her experience?

 ....

Connecting words: *although, even though, despite, in spite of, however* `V9.3`

3 **Rewrite sentences 1–6 in the article using the words in brackets.**

1 (even though) *Even though Ed Devlin had never cooked anything more than a burger, he beat three other professional chefs.*

2 (despite) ....

 ....

3 (however) ....

 ....

4 (however) ....

 ....

5 (although) ....

 ....

6 (in spite of) ....

 ....

Are you fed up with your job? Have you ever wanted to do something completely different? A top chef perhaps? Or maybe a racing driver or even a nightclub DJ? *Faking It* is a reality TV programme that does exactly that. The programme trains people to 'fake it' in a totally different job. They are given four weeks to learn the skills of their new jobs. Then they have to convince a group of experts that they aren't faking it.

Previous shows have taken a fast food worker and trained him as a top chef. [1]**Ed Devlin had never cooked anything more than a burger, but he beat three other professional chefs.** At the moment Ed is still doing the job he was doing before. However, he says he is much better at cutting up onions now!

Maximillian Devereaux, a professional chess player, learned how to be a football manager. [2]**He didn't manage to persuade* the experts, but he enjoyed the experience.** He thinks his body language at football matches wasn't good enough. "I never managed to look comfortable," he says.

Jatinder Sumal works in her family's newsagent's in Scotland. She learned to be a show business reporter! When a TV researcher phoned her and offered her the chance, Jatinder thought it was a joke. [3]**Although she had never heard of *Faking It*, her friends said it was a really good show.** So Jatinder thought she would have a go. Jatinder said the worst moment of her experience was at a film premiere. [4]**She tried to interview Robbie Williams, but she couldn't think of anything to ask him!** "I was very nervous," she said. "I couldn't stop shaking." [5]**It was a terrible experience, but Jatinder quickly recovered.** And at the end of her month's training, when she interviewed a pop group in front of the experts, they thought she was a genuine showbiz* reporter. [6]**Despite her success at 'faking it', Jatinder doesn't plan to leave her job.** "I wouldn't give up my life here in Glasgow for anything," she said. "I'm just glad to be back to my old life."

*persuade = make someone believe something
*showbiz = showbusiness

9D At the doctor's

Health problems, symptoms and treatment [V9.4]
At the doctor's [RW9.1]

1 Fill in the gaps with the words in brackets.

1 _Hay fever_ gives you a _____ nose and makes you _____ . (hay fever; sneeze; runny)

2 Food _____ can often make you _____ and give you _____ . (diarrhoea; poisoning; sick)

3 _____ is a type of _____ and is usually a _____ . (pill; painkiller; paracetamol)

4 A _____ of _____ is that you feel _____ . (wheezy; asthma; symptom)

5 If you have an _____ , a doctor will probably prescribe _____ . However, they don't work with a _____ . (infection; virus; antibiotics)

2 Put the conversation in the correct order.

a) **DOCTOR** Now, what seems to be the problem?
___1___

b) **DOCTOR** Doesn't it? It's very red. Do you know if you're allergic to anything? _____

c) **PATIENT** It doesn't hurt. _____

d) **PATIENT** I keep getting a rash on my arm. _____

e) **DOCTOR** Right, let me have a look at you. _____

f) **PATIENT** I'm allergic to cats, but we haven't got one. _____

3 a) Fill in the gaps with the words in the boxes.

| ~~feeling~~   suffering   getting (x 2)   taking |

a) I haven't been __feeling__ very well recently, doctor.

b) I keep _____ migraines in the morning.

c) Have you been _____ anything for them?

d) How long have you been _____ from them?

e) I'm _____ a sore throat.

| a prescription   some antibiotics   take them
another appointment   a week |

f) Come back if you're not feeling better in

_____ .

g) How often should I _____ ?

h) Here's a prescription for _____ .

i) Do I need to make _____ ?

j) Do I need _____ , doctor?

b) Complete the conversation with sentences a)–e) in 3a).

CASS ¹___a)___

²_____

DOCTOR I see. ³_____

CASS About a month or two.

DOCTOR Right. That's quite a long time. ⁴_____

CASS Paracetamol and aspirin.

DOCTOR OK. Painkillers are fine. Any other problems?

CASS Well … ⁵_____ today, but it's not serious.

c) Complete the conversation with sentences f)–j) in 3a).

BOB So you think it might be an infection.

⁶_____

DOCTOR Yes, I'm going to write one. ⁷_____

BOB Thanks a lot. ⁸_____

DOCTOR Twice a day, after meals.

BOB ⁹_____

DOCTOR No. ¹⁰_____

 Reading and Writing Portfolio 9 p80

Language Summary 10, Student's Book p136

10A The anniversary

Contacting people V10.1

1 Look at the photo. Choose the correct words in Bill and Jilly's conversation.

BILL   Hello! It's Jilly, isn't it?

JILLY   Bill! I haven't seen you since university!

BILL   That's right. [1](*Are you*)/*Do you get* in touch with people from then?

JILLY   Not really. I've [2]*kept in/lost* touch with almost everybody I think. And you?

BILL   Last year I [3]*got/got in* touch with someone who was on my course – I found her email address on the Internet. I even [4]*phoned/gave* her a call and [5]*left/posted* her a message.

JILLY   A girlfriend from the past?

BILL   You guessed it. She never [6]*called/called in* back.

JILLY   Oh, well. And your brother? You've [7]*kept in/lost* touch with him I hope!

BILL   Matt? He's here in London. You two went out once, didn't you?

JILLY   A long time ago ... when I used to hang about with that girl Susie.

BILL   Susie? Susie James?

JILLY   Yes, I'd love to [8]*find/get* hold of her. But I haven't a clue where she is now. I haven't heard [9]*of/from* her since she went to work in Spain.

BILL   Well, I [10]*got/'m* in touch with her – she's my sister-in-law!

JILLY   What?

BILL   Yes, in fact it's Matt and Susie's tenth wedding anniversary tomorrow.

JILLY   You're joking! Well, let them [11]*know/hear* I'm living in London now. Here's my card.

BILL   You're a divorce lawyer! Sounds fun!

was/were going to, was/were supposed to G10.1

2 Read sentence a). Then decide if statement b) is true (T) or false (F).

1   a) We weren't going to phone.
    b) [T] We phoned.

2   a) They weren't supposed to be here until seven.
    b) [ ] They arrived before seven.

3   a) We were supposed to pick up Carl, but we overslept.
    b) [ ] Carl was picked up.

4   a) Mike was going to get hold of the manager, but he forgot.
    b) [ ] Mike didn't get in touch with the manager.

5   a) We were going to catch the early train, but we missed it by a few minutes.
    b) [ ] They didn't catch the early train.

3 Choose the correct ending to the sentences. Sometimes both endings are possible.

1   I was going to give you a call,
   (a) but I didn't have enough time.
   b) and I left a message.

2   You were supposed to let them know
   a) and now they won't worry.
   b) that you weren't going to go.

3   He was supposed to give you my message,
   a) but you didn't call me back.
   b) but I guess he forgot.

4   Sandy and I weren't going to come
   a) but we're glad we did.
   b) because we didn't think we were invited.

5   It was supposed to be sunny today,
   a) however, it looks like it's going to rain.
   b) so perhaps this rain will stop soon.

4 **a)** Match beginnings of sentences 1–8 to endings a)–h).

1 We had planned to go to bed early, but ___c)___

2 I didn't ask for a big room, but _____

3 I'd thought about having a party that weekend, but _____

4 Someone had asked me to invite him, but _____

5 We had expected the concert to end at nine, but _____

6 No one had planned to give them anything, but _____

7 We had arranged to meet in the morning, but _____

8 I was told to get in touch with Diana, but _____

a) then they heard it was for charity.

b) it's already half past.

c) Mike gave us free tickets to a concert.

d) it's good that it is.

e) Cath rang earlier and made an excuse.

f) I didn't know you were going to be on holiday.

g) her phone number had changed.

h) I knew he wouldn't come.

b) Rewrite beginnings of sentences 1–8 in **4a)** using the correct form of *was/were going to* or *was/were supposed to*.

1 We _were going to go to bed early, but ..._

2 The room _____

3 I _____

4 I _____

5 The concert _____

6 No one _____

7 We _____

8 I _____

 Who's that?

Describing people V10.2

1 **a)** Correct the two mistakes in each description.

    in
1 Oscar is ~~on~~ his late fifties. He's got glasses and he's going to bald.

2 Chris is in his mid-thirties. He's got dark short hair and striped shirt.

3 Erin is Maisie's twin. She's got straight blonde hairs and a dress flowery.

4 Alice is in her mid-fifties. She's got some length-shoulder hair and a light jacket.

b) Read the descriptions in **1a)** again. Write the names of people a)–d) on the picture.

2 Look at the picture. Complete the sentences.

1 Describe these people's hair.

a) Kian's hair _is short and curly._

b) Jay's hair _____

_____

c) Fern's hair _____

_____

2 Describe the differences between what these people are wearing.

a) Fern has got _dark trousers._

Alice has got _____

b) Chris has got _____

Oscar has got _____

Modal verbs (2): making deductions G10.2

3 **a)** **Make sentences with these words.**

1 use / must / hair straighteners / Eve .
   Eve must use hair straighteners.

2 with / Ruby / be / ponytail/ could / the / The girl .
   ....

3 stuck / be / Jo / in traffic / could .
   ....

4 be / later / party / might / Joel / to the / coming .
   ....

5 must / leaving / in a / Stephen / minute / be .
   ....

6 may / at home / stay / The children / to / prefer .
   ....

7 can't / any worse / weather / The / get .
   ....

8 working / be / Simon / there any more / can't .
   ....

b) **Read the sentences in 3a) again. Are these sentences true (T) or false (F)?**

The speaker ...

1 [T] believes Eve uses hair straighteners.
2 [ ] knows who Ruby is.
3 [ ] thinks Jo is possibly stuck in traffic.
4 [ ] doesn't know if Joel is coming to the party.
5 [ ] is sure that Stephen is leaving soon.
6 [ ] thinks the children definitely want to stay at home.
7 [ ] thinks the weather isn't very good.
8 [ ] isn't sure whether Simon has left his old job.

4 **a)** **Look at the picture on page 51 again and fill in the gaps with the words in the boxes.**

~~can't~~ must may

PHOEBE Chris looks absolutely exhausted. Jamie [1] *can't* be sleeping very well.

LEO Yes. And Jamie's crying a lot. He [2] .... need something to eat.

PHOEBE Or he [3] .... be tired, perhaps?

LEO You're probably right. But I don't think I'll point that out to Chris!

must could can't

LEO I'm not sure, but Oscar's new girlfriend [4] .... be the woman with sunglasses.

PHOEBE Well she [5] .... be the one with curly hair. She's my age!

LEO No. She [6] .... have lots of money. Look at all that jewellery!

can't must might

PHOEBE Kian came with his parents. I'm not sure but he [7] .... be working with his dad again. Who's the girl near him?

LEO I think her name's Fern.

PHOEBE Oh, she [8] .... be Kian's girlfriend. I've heard him speak about her.

LEO Then Kian [9] .... be working with his dad. She said she works in the same office as her boyfriend.

b) **Write sentences using *must*, *could*, *may*, *might* or *can't*. Sometimes more than one verb is possible.**

1 Jamie / be / feel / hungry or tired.
   Jamie might be feeling hungry or tired.

2 Jamie / be Chris's son.
   Jamie must be Chris's son.

3 Phoebe / be / have / a baby soon.
   ....

4 Leo / be Phoebe's grandfather.
   ....

5 Chris / be / stay / at the party until late.
   ....

6 Phoebe and Leo / get on well.
   ....

7 Erin and Maisie / be / chat / about Oscar.
   ....

8 Jay / be retired yet.
   ....

10C The party's over

Phrasal verbs (3): meanings and grammar V10.3 V10.4

1 **Read the article. Then fill in the gaps with sentences a)–e).**

a) he was younger
b) I had hardly eaten anything
c) you don't tend to worry about things for long
d) ~~I was still surprised~~
e) my brother was actually going to get married

Being a best man by Oliver Pedoe

"I'd like you to be my best man," said my brother.

Even though my brother and I had always got on well and rarely a)**argued**, ¹ _I was still surprised_ . I was only just 18. I had only been to a few weddings in my life and I was already going to be a best man. I accepted immediately – it was more evidence that I was becoming an adult. At last.

During dinner that evening, my mother b)**told me** that best men were, of course, supposed to make speeches.

"Supposed to or have to?" I asked, feeling my heart rate* c)**increasing** a little.

"Well, have to," she said.

Suddenly I didn't feel hungry any more.

There wasn't any point in trying to d)**avoid doing it**. And of course when you're young, ² ....
I started making excuses to myself so I could e)**do it later**: after all, my brother and his fiancée might f)**end their relationship** and the wedding would be cancelled.

A week before the wedding it was clear that ³ ....
.... I needed a speech. Quickly.

I g)**searched for** wedding speeches in the place which seems to have the answers to everything: the Internet. After a few minutes I h)**found** a website with tips on making speeches. It suggested finding photos of the groom when ⁴ ....

Perfect! There were hundreds of photos of my brother when he was young: my brother as a baby, my brother with his first 'girlfriend', my brother with long hair, my brother with short hair and a beard. Easy.

When the moment finally arrived, I can't say I wasn't nervous. Wedding speeches are made after a meal and ⁵ ....
.... However, within a few minutes of standing up to make my speech, I started to i)**feel better about it**. The photos were a huge success and everyone was asking how I j)**had thought of** such an original idea. Of course I lied. More evidence I was becoming an adult. At last.

heart rate = the speed at which your heart beats

2 **Rewrite words/phrases a)–j) in bold in the article using the correct form of these phrasal verbs.**

> point out   get out of it
> come up with   look up
> come across   go up
> split up   get over it
> ~~fall out~~   put it off

a) ... _fell out_ ...

b) ....

c) ....

d) ....

e) ....

f) ....

g) ....

h) ....

i) ....

j) ....

3 **Are these sentences true (T) or false (F)?**

1 [T] Oliver was 18 when his brother asked him to be his best man.

2 [ ] He had been a best man before.

3 [ ] He knew a best man had to make a speech when he accepted.

4 [ ] He didn't try to avoid having to make a speech.

5 [ ] He was sure his brother was going to split up with his fiancée.

6 [ ] It was Oliver's own idea to use photos for his speech.

7 [ ] At the wedding, Oliver was nervous at first.

8 [ ] Oliver told everyone where he got the idea for his speech.

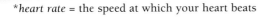

10D Do you mind?

Asking for, giving and refusing permission

1 Read the situations. Then choose the correct questions and sentences.

1 Your teacher has forgotten her pen. She asks:
   a) Is it OK if you use a pen?
   b) Would you mind if I used my pen?
   c) Do you think I could use your pen?

2 You give her permission. You say:
   a) Yes, I'd rather you didn't.
   b) Yes, of course you can. Go ahead.
   c) Yes, of course it is.

3 You want to borrow some money from a friend. You ask:
   a) Would you mind if I borrowed some money from you?
   b) Is it OK if I lend you some money?
   c) Would you like to borrow some money?

4 Your friend gives you permission. Your friend says:
   a) Yes, I'd rather you didn't.
   b) No, not at all.
   c) Yes, of course.

2 Read the short conversations and choose the correct words. Sometimes more than one answer is correct.

1 A *Do you mind if*/*Do you think* I do the washing-up later?
   B *Yes, go ahead.*/*No, do whatever you like.*

2 A *May*/*Can* I borrow your bike?
   B *No, take whatever you like.*/*Yes, help yourself.*

3 A *Is it OK if*/*Do you think* I change the channel?
   B *Of course.*/*I'm afraid I'm watching this.*

4 A *Is it OK*/*Would you mind if* Mike stayed here this evening?
   B *I'd rather he didn't.*/*Go ahead!*

5 A *Could*/*May* I put our meeting off for a week?
   B *I'd rather you didn't.*/*Yes, sure.*

6 A *Do you think*/*Do you mind* I could use your bathroom?
   B *Yes, of course.*/*No, not at all.*

3 **a)** You are staying at a friend's house. Write questions with these words to ask for permission.

1 May / borrow / a towel?
   May I borrow a towel?

2 Do you think / have / a glass?
   _____

3 Is it OK / make / some coffee?
   _____

4 Can / look round / your garden?
   _____

5 Would / mind / check / my email?
   _____

6 Do / mind / have / a shower?
   _____

b) Use one of these phrases to complete the replies to the questions in **3a)**.

| ~~Yes, of course~~   Yes, of course it is   Sorry, you can't |
| No, not at all   Go ahead   Yes, of course you can |

1 *Yes, of course* . I'll just get one.

2 _____ . I'll just wash one up.

3 _____ . Help yourself to anything you want.

4 _____ . It's a bit of a mess, though.

5 _____ . There's something wrong with the laptop at the moment.

6 _____ . Use my hair dryer if you want.

 Reading and Writing Portfolio 10 p82

11 All part of the job

Language Summary 11, Student's Book p138

11A Any messages?

Things people do at work V11.1

1 Cathy is telling her boss why she wants to leave. Complete her boss's notes with the correct form of these verbs.

~~have~~ do get sort spend work go be organise

Cathy Pepper – conference assistant
Reasons for wanting to leave

- She ¹ _has_ too much responsibility and it's making her feel stressed.
- Nobody ² _____ out as many problems as she does.
- She ³ _____ in charge of the company for a month last May!
- She has ⁴ _____ two conferences by herself.
- She can't stand ⁵ _____ shifts any more.
- She ⁶ _____ a lot of unpaid overtime last month.
- She must ⁷ _____ more time with her family.
- She's ⁸ _____ for an audition next week for an acting job!
- She'll ⁹ _____ in touch after the audition.

2 Fill in the gaps in the advertisement for Cathy's old job with these words.

~~conferences~~ responsible department shifts
overtime deadlines problems

Conference assistant

- Have you organised company ¹ _conferences_ ?
- Can you sort out difficult ² _____ and find solutions quickly?
- Are you good at meeting ³ _____ ?
- Are you able to work ⁴ _____ and do ⁵ _____ when necessary?

If you can answer *yes* to these questions, you might be the person we're looking for. You will be ⁶ _____ for company conferences as part of a team. The ⁷ _____ is run at our London office.

Call Kristan Halsey on 020 8348 472 for an application form.

Reported speech: sentences G11.1

3 Match sentences 1–7 to reported speech sentences a)–f). You need to use one sentence a)–f) twice.

1 I'm leaving my job. __c)__
2 I've left my job. _____
3 I left my job. _____
4 I am going to leave my job. _____
5 I'll leave my job. _____
6 I can leave my job. _____
7 I must leave my job. _____

She said ...
a) she had to leave her job.
b) she had left her job.
c) she was leaving her job.
d) she could leave her job.
e) she would leave her job.
f) she was going to leave her job.

4 Cathy's colleagues are discussing why she left. Read the reasons in **1** and complete the reported speech sentences.

1 Cathy said _she had too much responsibility_ .
2 She said nobody _____ .
3 She told me _____ .
4 She said _____ .
5 She said _____ .
6 She told me _____ .
7 She said _____ .
8 She said _____ .
9 She told me _____ .

5 Look at the messages and write reported sentences. Use *tell* and the correct object (*her*, *him* or *them*).

1 Vic *told him she couldn't find his email about the conference.*

2 Sally's husband ....

....

3 The receptionist ....

....

4 Cathy ....

....

1
Message for: *Thomas*
From: *Vic*
She can't find your email about the conference.

2
Message for: *Sally*
From: *Your husband*
He doesn't have to work tonight so he's going to pick up the children from school.

3
Message for: *Simon*
From: *Receptionist (at the dentist's)*
The dentist isn't well today so you must call to rearrange your appointment.

4
Message for: *Kristan and Dan*
From: *Cathy*
She'll be at home this afternoon if you want to ring her.

11B How did it go?

Adjectives to describe jobs V11.2

1 Read the description and complete the crossword.

People think that being an actor is quite (9→) *glamorous* – all those parties and premieres. And of course, premieres are exciting evenings – it's incredibly (10→) .... to see the result of all your hard work. But on film or TV sets, you have to wait around for long periods of time. It can actually be quite (3↓) .... I'd like to be a (12→) .... actor, but I don't have enough work. Also I can't take a (8→) .... job because I might have to leave at any time. Acting is quite (4↓) .... , but I've got a lot of bills to pay! So, in the afternoons, I have a (6↓) .... job in an office. The work isn't difficult. In fact, I wouldn't want anything too (1↓) .... I need to be awake in the evenings to learn my lines! I can't imagine doing an everyday job – it's too (7↓) .... for me. Acting isn't (5→) .... at all. But earning enough to live can be. My office job isn't (2→) .... , but it's only (11→) .... I'm just waiting for a lucky break!

Reported speech: questions G11.2

2 a) Isabel has just had an interview for a job looking after a couple's children in Edinburgh. Match beginnings 1–10 to endings a)–j) of the questions she was asked.

1 How many jobs have ....*i)*....

2 Are you living ....

3 What will you do if ....

4 Did you ....

5 What was your ....

6 Have you ever ....

7 Does anyone in your ....

8 How many people ....

9 Will you email ....

10 How long are ....

a) us your referee's phone number?

b) in Scotland at the moment?

c) family live in the UK?

d) you planning to stay in the UK?

e) last job?

f) do you know in Edinburgh?

g) you don't get this job?

h) looked after twins before?

i) you applied for?

j) look after children in Spain?

Crossword grid:

9 across: G L A M O R O U S

b) Isabel is telling a friend about the interview. Read the reported questions and choose the correct words.

1 They asked me how many jobs *(I)/you* had applied for.

2 They asked me *if I/I* was living in Scotland at the moment.

3 They wanted to know what I *will/would* do if I *didn't get/hadn't got* this job.

4 They asked me whether I *had looked/looked* after children in Spain.

5 They wanted to know what *was my last job/ my last job was*.

c) Write questions 6–10 in **2a)** in reported speech.

6 They asked me if I *had ever looked after twins before.*

7 ....

....

8 ....

....

9 ....

....

10 ....

Reported speech: requests and imperatives G11.3

3 Carlos has an English speaking exam. Look at the picture and write his teachers' and friend's sentences in reported speech.

1 Don't chew gum!

2 Use plenty of vocabulary.

3 Don't get nervous.

4 Speak clearly.

5 Listen to the questions carefully.

6 Don't be late.

7 Could you check the time of my exam?

8 Can you tell me the questions later?

1 *She told Carlos not to chew gum.*

2 ....

3 ....

4 ....

5 ....

6 ....

7 ....

....

8 ....

11C Undercover

Confessions of a parking attendant

The job of a parking attendant (PA) is not a rewarding one. They have to walk about 25 kilometres every day, in all weather conditions. Drivers sometimes threaten [1] _to hurt PAs_ (hurt; PAs) when they are given tickets. And there are about three physical attacks on PAs every day – just in London.

However, when an undercover reporter from the BBC applied for a job as a PA, he discovered illegal tickets, bribes* and theft. For six months Nkem Ifejika worked undercover as a PA. During the training bosses frequently reminded [2] _____ (him; give out) as many tickets as possible. New PAs must give drivers at least 10 tickets every day to pass their training.

In his first few months, Nkem found it difficult to give out enough tickets. Bosses warned [3] _____ _____ (him; improve) or he would lose his job. But then PAs offered [4] _____ (tell; Nkem) how to increase the amount of fines he gave. They suggested [5] _____ (give; tickets) to abandoned* cars and waiting in car parks until cars were parked illegally.

Another BBC reporter, working undercover as a taxi driver, also met a PA who agreed [6] _____ _____ _____ (cancel; parking tickets) for half the price of the fine. The PA used stolen credit cards to pay the fine and then collected the bribe from the driver. The PA didn't admit [7] _____ (steal; credit cards). He said he invented the numbers.

When the BBC told the parking companies about the reporters' experiences, they promised [8] _____ _____ (investigate; the problem) and report anything illegal to the police. However, they refused [9] _____ (believe; the problem) was serious. And Nkem says himself, "the vast* majority of parking attendants are honest and hard-working."

However, it seems clear that some are not.

Adapted from *Confessions of a Parking Attendant* BBC News 1/06/05

bribe = money or a present that you give to someone so that they will do something (usually dishonest)
abandoned = left in a place permanently because you don't want it any more.
vast = extremely big

Reporting verbs `V11.3` Verb patterns (2): reporting verbs `V11.4`

1 Read the article quickly and choose the best statement.

a) Nkem is an honest parking attendant who decided to contact the BBC.
b) Nkem became a parking attendant to investigate illegal fines for the BBC.
c) Nkem is a dishonest parking attendant who was discovered by the BBC.

2 Read the article again. Fill in the gaps with the correct form of the verb and the object in brackets.

3 Answer the questions.

1 Why is a parking attendant's job difficult?

_____

2 Why did Nkem get a job as a parking attendant?

_____

3 Why did Nkem almost lose his job?

_____

4 What did one parking attendant use to cancel fines?

_____

5 What did the parking companies think about Nkem's report?

_____

11D **It's my first day**

Checking information RW11.1

1 a) Match sentences 1–6 to replies a)–f).

1 Can you give that number to me again, please? ....*a)*....

2 And could you tell me your surname again? ....

3 Is that spelt W–E–S–T? ....

4 Is that spelt Steven with a V? ....

5 Sorry, what did you say his name was again? ....

6 Do you mean Terry Jones? ....

a) Of course. It's 020 72898016.
b) That's it. As in North, South, etc.
c) No, Alex. Terry's younger brother.
d) Mine? It's Newman. N–E–W–M–A–N.
e) No, with a PH.
f) It's Jones. Terry Jones. I think he works in the finance department.

b) Which conversations in 1a) ask someone to repeat information and which ones check information?

Ask someone to repeat information:

....*1*.... , ... , ...

Check information:

.... , ... , ...

2 Put the sentences in the conversation in the correct order.

a) [1] PAUL I'm ringing about Mr Newman's lunch meeting with Ms Bennis. I'm afraid Ms Bennis has to cancel.

b) [ ] PAUL No, double T.

c) [ ] PAUL Sorry. I said Ms Bennis isn't well today.

d) [ ] PAUL Yes, it was today at 1 p.m. I'm sorry for the late notice. Ms Bennis isn't well.

e) [ ] PAUL My name? I'm Paul Cutt. Ms Bennis's personal secretary.

f) [ ] ROSE Oh, dear. I hope she's better soon. What did you say your name was again?

g) [ ] ROSE Is that spelt C–U–T?

h) [ ] ROSE Sorry, I didn't quite catch that.

i) [ ] ROSE Cancel? OK. Let me check Mr Newman's diary. Do you mean today's lunch meeting?

j) [ ] ROSE OK, thanks Paul. I'll let Mr Newman know. Bye!

3 Fill in the gaps in the conversation with the phrases in the boxes.

| get all of that | give it to |
| tell me | say that | is that |

BOB The address is 19 Sutherland Lane, Rainham, Kent ME16 8VD.

GILL Sorry, I didn't ¹ _get all of that_ . Can you ² .... me again? 19 South Land …

BOB Sutherland Lane, Rainham, Kent ME16 8VD.

GILL Sorry, could you ³ .... postcode again? Um, ⁴ .... 8BD?

BOB No, 8VD. V for Victor.

GILL Thanks. And could you ⁵ .... your name again?

BOB Yes, of course. It's Bob Smith.

GILL Thanks. That's nice and easy.

| is that | what did you say | is your |
| do you mean | are you talking | I didn't |

SARA Hi. It's Sara Caperski here. Can I speak to Alan David, please?

GILL Sorry, ⁶ .... quite catch that. Was it Alan David?

SARA Yes. He's responsible for the conference.

GILL So ⁷ .... about the London or Birmingham conference?

SARA The London one.

GILL Oh, ⁸ .... David Allen?

SARA Yes, of course. Sorry.

GILL That's OK. Sorry, ⁹ .... your name was again?

SARA Sara Caperski.

GILL And ¹⁰ .... Sarah with an H?

SARA No, no H.

GILL And ¹¹ .... surname spelt C–A–P–E–R–S–K–I?

SARA That's right.

 Reading and Writing Portfolio 11 p84

59

12 Real or imaginary

Language Summary 12, Student's Book p140

 I wish!

Informal words and phrases `V12.1`

 1 **a)** Make sentences with these words.

1 you / Do / out later / going / fancy ?

   Do you fancy going out later?

2 I'm / clubs / really into / not .

   ....

3 solution / reckon there's / simple / I / a .

   ....

4 no / of / sick / having / I'm / money .

   ....

5 it tonight / I / up / don't feel / to .

   ....

6 of the / month / broke until / I'm / the end .

   ....

b) Fill in gaps a)–f) in the conversation with sentences 1–6 in **1a)**.

JESS   a) *Do you fancy going out later?*

      We're going to a club.

KIRSTY   No, thanks. b) ....

JESS   What? Are you serious? You love clubs.

KIRSTY   Yes, but c) ....

JESS   That doesn't sound like you. What's wrong?

KIRSTY   d) ....

JESS   Again? This happens every month.

KIRSTY   I know. e) ....

JESS   f) ....

      Spend less than you earn!

2 Rewrite the words/phrases in **bold** with the correct form of these informal expressions.

> ~~not be up to (someone)~~   be off   hang around
> have a go at (doing something)   could do with
> can't be bothered (to do something)

1 Well, it**'s not my decision**!

   Well, it's not up to me!

2 **I'm not interested in doing** the washing-up tonight.

   ....

3 **Are** you **going?**

   ....

4 Why **are** you **waiting around?**

   ....

5 I want to **try** starting my own website.

   ....

6 I **need** a shower.

   ....

Wishes `G12.1`

 3 Fill in the gaps with the correct form of the verbs in brackets.

1 We don't feel up to going.

   We wish we ___*felt*___ (feel) up to going.

2 It's rains almost every day.

   I wish it .... (not rain) so much.

3 Mo can't get to sleep.

   She wishes she .... (can) get to sleep.

4 I'm badly paid.

   I wish I .... (be) better paid.

5 They are leaving tomorrow.

   I wish they .... (stay) longer.

6 We're doing dull jobs.

   We wish we .... (do) more interesting and challenging work.

4 **a)** Write sentences with *wish* for these situations.

1 I have to work full-time.

   I wish *I didn't have to work full-time* .

2 I can't go.

   I wish ....

3 They're wearing jeans and trainers.

   I wish ....

4 I don't know how to drive.

   I wish ....

5 I have to leave early.

   I wish ....

6 I'm so tired.

   I wish ....

b) Choose the correct words.

a) I *saw*/*'d see* more of my children if I *could*/*would be able to* work less.

b) I *didn't*/*wouldn't* have to pay for taxis, if I *were able to/ would* drive.

c) If I *would*/*could* stay later, we *could*/*would be able to* talk for longer.

d) *Would*/*Did* you go, if I *could*/*would* go?

e) If they *would be*/*were* dressed better, they *looked*/*would look* a lot more professional.

f) I *met*/*would meet* you tonight, if I *wouldn't*/*didn't* feel so exhausted.

c) Match the wishes in **4a)** to the sentences in **4b)**.

1 ....*a)*....   3 ....   5 ....

2 ....   4 ....   6 ....

12B Important moments

Phrases with *get* V12.2

1 **a)** Match beginnings of sentences 1–9 to endings a)–i).

1 My husband's Spanish, so he gets ....*g)*....

2 If we had a GPS, we wouldn't get ....

3 I don't know when he got ....

4 Can you do the washing-up when you get ....

5 During the day we get ....

6 If he doesn't have enough sleep, he gets ....

7 Is it tomorrow or Sunday that Simon gets ....

8 That sound on my phone means I've got ....

9 When I left work, I got ....

a) angry at the tiniest problem.

b) to work, but it must have been late.

c) a text message.

d) home from work this evening?

e) a lot of presents from my colleagues.

f) a lot of phone calls trying to sell us stuff.

g) fed up with the weather in England.

h) lost, would we?

i) back from his holiday?

b) Match the sentences in **1a)** to the different meanings of *get*.

a) receive/obtain: ....*5*.... , ... , ...

b) travel/arrive: .... , ... , ...

c) become: .... , ... , ...

2 Complete the sentences with the correct form of *get* and these words/phrases.

~~something to drink~~	into trouble	around	here
in touch with	older	rid of	the job

1 It's so humid, isn't it? Gary's gone *to get something to drink* .

2 I haven't seen Jess since last December. I must .... her soon.

3 I wouldn't touch that if I were you. Mark did, and he ....

4 Will and Luke haven't arrived yet. In fact, if they .... before seven, I'd be surprised.

5 I hardly ever take a taxi when I'm abroad. I prefer .... by bus.

6 What does the letter say, Michelle? Have you .... ?

7 I can't move as quickly as I used to. I guess I'm just ....

8 We're .... this sofa soon if you want it. You just have to pick it up.

Third conditional G12.2

 3 **a) Choose the correct words.**

1 If they *wouldn't have*/~~hadn't~~ got lost, they'd *arrived*/~~have arrived~~ on time.

2 Ken *would have/had* rung her if he'd *have got/got* the message.

3 If he *wouldn't have/hadn't* got to work late again, he *hadn't/wouldn't have* got sacked.

4 Kat and Jo *hadn't/wouldn't have* gone to the film if they'd *have/'d* seen the review.

5 If Sue *hadn't/wouldn't have* got in touch with me, I *wouldn't have/hadn't* known Vi wasn't well.

6 We *hadn't/wouldn't have* got home if he *hadn't/wouldn't have* given us a lift.

b) Read the sentences in 3a) again and answer these questions.

1 a) Did they get lost? *Yes.*
  b) Did they arrive late? ....

2 a) Did Ken get the message? ....
  b) Did Ken phone her? ....

3 a) Did Tony arrive on time? ....
  b) Did he lose his job? ....

4 a) Did they read the review? ....
  b) Did they see the film? ....

5 a) Did Sue get in touch? ....
  b) Did Sue tell me Vi was ill? ....

6 a) Did we get home? ....
  b) Did he give us a lift? ....

4 **Fill in the gaps with the correct form of these pairs of verbs.**

> ~~score / not lose~~   not get / have
> leave / fail   met / not be
> not see / not buy   not be / let
> get / get   not encourage / not become

1 If I *had scored* the penalty, we *wouldn't have lost* .

2 We .... never .... if we .... on the same flight.

3 If they .... to know each other, they .... on.

4 I .... the job advert if I .... a newspaper that day.

5 If my parents .... me, I .... a surgeon.

6 I .... worried if you .... me know.

7 If I .... your phone call, I .... the meeting.

8 He .... university if he .... the exam.

5 **a) Fill in the gaps in the story with these verbs.**

> get   asked   took
> got (x 2)   split up   had
> started   felt   went

Thirty years ago Jodie was going out with a boy called Callum. On her birthday, Callum didn't [1] *get* her a present and Jodie [2] .... really angry. They [3] .... a huge argument and [4] .... That night she [5] .... out with some friends because she [6] .... upset. At the end of the evening, she [7] .... a taxi because the underground had closed. The taxi driver was really friendly so they [8] .... talking. They [9] .... on so well that the taxi driver [10] .... her for her phone number. Who was Jodie? My mother! And the taxi driver? My father, of course!

b) Read the story again and complete the conditional sentences.

1 If Callum *had got* her a present, Jodie *wouldn't have got* really angry.

2 They .... stayed together if they .... an argument.

3 If she .... upset, she .... with her friends.

4 If she .... home earlier, the underground .... open.

5 She .... a taxi if the underground had .... open.

6 If the taxi driver .... so friendly, they .... started talking.

7 The taxi driver .... her for her number if they .... so well.

8 If she .... him her number, I would never have been born!

12C Superheroes

1 Read the article quickly and match headings 1–5 with paragraphs A–E.

1 A different kind of superhero ___C___   4 An important moment _____

2 Stan's most famous superhero _____   5 After Marvel Comics _____

3 How Lieberman became Lee _____

Word formation (3): word families (1) and (2) `V12.3` `V12.4`

2 Fill in the gaps in the article with the correct form of the words in brackets. Use a verb, noun or adjective.

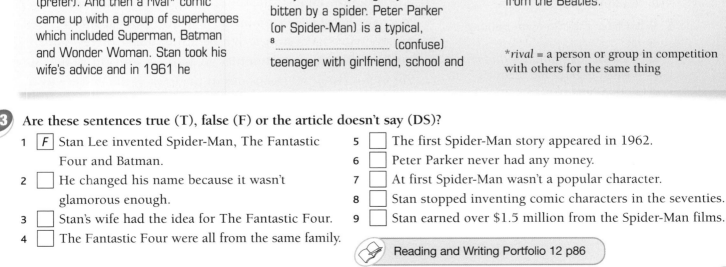

Super-Stan!

A Stan Lieberman was born in New York in 1922. He joined the family publishing business, Timely Publications, in 1939. Stan had a fantastic ¹ _imagination_ (imagine) and for the next twenty years, Stan wrote thousands of ² _____ (entertain) crime, science fiction and western stories for Timely. Characters were either good or bad – and stories rarely used words with more than two syllables. In fact, Stan was so ³ _____ (embarrass) by what he was writing that he used the name 'Stan Lee' in the comics.

B By 40, Stan had decided he was too old to write comics. His wife suggested writing stories about the things he ⁴ _____ (prefer). And then a rival* comic came up with a group of superheroes which included Superman, Batman and Wonder Woman. Stan took his wife's advice and in 1961 he

⁵ _____ (create) The Fantastic Four with the cartoonist, Jack Kirby.

C Until that time, superheroes had been 'perfect' people. And for Stan, their adventures were ⁶ _____ (predict) because nobody could hurt them. The Fantastic Four were different. The group had the same problems we all have. Two characters were engaged and they often fell out, for example. Another character was always depressed. The Fantastic Four were a huge success and Stan's ⁷ _____ (create) was back.

D A year later Stan and cartoonist Steve Ditko published their first story about a young boy who was bitten by a spider. Peter Parker (or Spider-Man) is a typical, ⁸ _____ (confuse) teenager with girlfriend, school and

money problems. The character was immediately ⁹ _____ (succeed). A copy of the first Spider-Man comic in good condition now costs about $30,000.

E In the early seventies Lee finally retired from publishing comics. The company – now called Marvel Comics – had become the most ¹⁰ _____ (success) comic book publisher in the world and was selling 50 million comics a year. Recently Stan has had small ¹¹ _____ (act) roles in *The Simpsons* and the Spider-Man films – which have earned over $1.6 billion in ticket sales. And at the moment he is planning new heroes – including a cartoon whose voice will be provided by Ringo Starr from the Beatles.

*rival = a person or group in competition with others for the same thing

3 Are these sentences true (T), false (F) or the article doesn't say (DS)?

1 [F] Stan Lee invented Spider-Man, The Fantastic Four and Batman.

2 [ ] He changed his name because it wasn't glamorous enough.

3 [ ] Stan's wife had the idea for The Fantastic Four.

4 [ ] The Fantastic Four were all from the same family.

5 [ ] The first Spider-Man story appeared in 1962.

6 [ ] Peter Parker never had any money.

7 [ ] At first Spider-Man wasn't a popular character.

8 [ ] Stan stopped inventing comic characters in the seventies.

9 [ ] Stan earned over $1.5 million from the Spider-Man films.

✎ Reading and Writing Portfolio 12 p86

Reading and Writing Portfolio 1

Describing a holiday

Reading a letter about a holiday
Writing informal letters: ellipsis of words
Review Past Simple; likes and dislikes

 Read the letter quickly.

a) Who is the letter to?

....

b) Who is the letter from?

....

c) What is the writer doing?

....

 Read the letter and choose the best answers.

1 Who is Anna travelling with?
 a) David and her children.
 b) David's grandparents.
 c) Her parents.

2 Which places have they been to so far?
 a) New York.
 b) New York and Boston.
 c) New York, Boston and Province Town.

3 What annoys David?
 a) He prefers cities.
 b) His grandparents have dinner very early.
 c) The traffic in New York.

4 When did they stay in New Hampshire?
 a) Between Boston and Cape Cod.
 b) Between New York and Boston.
 c) Between Boston and Cambridge.

5 What have they done on holiday so far?
 a) Had friends round for dinner.
 b) Visited friends and relatives.
 c) Both a) and b).

6 Why did the children stop exploring the woods?
 a) Because there were bears in there.
 b) Because their father told them to.
 c) Because they were scared.

De......

¹**Writing this in the car**. We're driving to Province Town, a beach town near Cape Cod in Massachusetts. We're in the second week of our two weeks away. And so far, Mum, it's been really special. We spent two days in New York. ²**Hotel was a bit basic but it was safe and clean**. We went to a few exhibitions and Simon and Ailsa had us round for lunch – you remember our neighbours from Oxford, don't you? NY is a wonderful place – really exciting. The traffic got on my nerves after a while – ³**worse than Cambridge!**

⁴**Tuesday we drove up to New Hampshire**. On the way, we said a quick 'hello' to David's grandparents near Boston. And we're going to go back and stay with them later in the week. They're well. They have dinner at about 4 p.m. these days – ⁵**drives David crazy!**

I can't normally bear the country, Mum. You know me – I'm a city girl. But New Hampshire is so quiet and so green – I fell in love with it. We stayed in a beautiful house there – some friend of David's grandmother owns it. Eve and Harry had a lot of fun exploring the woods at the back of the house – until David told them there might be some bears in there! Then they wouldn't go back again!

⁶**Will write again before we come home.**

Love,

Anna, David, Eve and Harry

Help with Writing Informal letters: ellipsis of words

3 **a)** We sometimes miss out words in informal writing when it is clear what or who we are talking about. Look at this sentence from the letter.

I'm Writing this in the car.

b) What types of words are missed out in sentences 1–6 in **bold** in the letter?

1 *pronoun and auxiliary verb*

2 ⎯⎯⎯⎯⎯⎯⎯⎯⎯⎯⎯⎯

3 ⎯⎯⎯⎯⎯⎯⎯⎯⎯⎯⎯⎯

4 ⎯⎯⎯⎯⎯⎯⎯⎯⎯⎯⎯⎯

5 ⎯⎯⎯⎯⎯⎯⎯⎯⎯⎯⎯⎯

6 ⎯⎯⎯⎯⎯⎯⎯⎯⎯⎯⎯⎯

c) Match words a)–f) to answers 1–6 in **3b)**.

a) I'm ___1___

b) I ⎯⎯⎯⎯

c) it's ⎯⎯⎯⎯

d) The ⎯⎯⎯⎯

e) it ⎯⎯⎯⎯

f) On ⎯⎯⎯⎯

4 Cross out the words you can miss out in these sentences.

1 ~~The~~ queue is so long. (1 word)
2 In August Sally and I are going to Washington. (1 word)
3 I can't find the map. (2 words)
4 I have not got any money! (2 words)
5 Have you had a lie-in today? (2 words)
6 We have been out for dinner. (2 words)
7 It is going to be sunny tomorrow. (2 words)
8 We are going to Al's tonight. (2 words)

5 **a)** Imagine you are on holiday for two weeks. Make notes on your own ideas in the diary.

Mon 1	Leave home. Fly to ⎯⎯⎯⎯	Mon 8	
Tue 2	Stay with ⎯⎯⎯⎯	Tue 9	Go to ⎯⎯⎯⎯
Wed 3		Wed 10	
Thur 4	Leave for ⎯⎯⎯⎯ by ⎯⎯⎯⎯	Thur 11	
Fri 5		Fri 12	
Sat 6	Visit ⎯⎯⎯⎯	Sat 13	Go back to ⎯⎯⎯⎯ by ⎯⎯⎯⎯
Sun 7		Sun 14	⎯⎯⎯⎯

b) Write a letter to a family member on Monday 8th.

- Use your notes from **5a)**.
- Add information about what you liked and didn't like during the first week of your holiday.
- Organise your letter into paragraphs.
- Use ellipsis of words where possible.
- Read and check for mistakes.
- Give your letter to your teacher next class.

Tick the things you can do in English in the Reading and Writing Progress Portfolio, p88.

Notices at work

Reading notices
Writing notices: abbreviations
Review modal verbs

1 Read notices A–F and sentences a)–e). Which notice or notices would each person be interested in?

a) TOM — I ought to do more exercise. __A__ , _____

b) EVA — I have to get a part-time job. _____

c) MARK — I found something in a classroom recently. _____

d) SALLY — I lost something recently. _____

e) VICTORIA — I have to find some accommodation before university starts. _____

A

Man's bike for sale
6 months old – vgc
£150 ono (for quick sale!)
Call Mike on
07912 004121

B

Cleaner needed
Private house in Percy St.

No experience necessary.

£7 **p/h**, 3 hours **p/w**

nancy@ukmail.net

C

Lost

Red bag in class 7B on Wednesday.

Pls. help! It's got all my notes in it.

Carla 07980 545618

D

Room to let
In friendly shared house near college. Available from 1st October.

£90 **p/w** + bills

n/s only

room_for_rent@ukmail.net

E

Yoga class
8-week beginners' course in sports centre.

7–8.30 p.m.
Mondays and Thursdays.

Call Sue
Tel. no. 01222 641813
(**eves.** only)

F

FOUND
Mobile phone in room 4A.
Nokia 332 (black).
Last **Tue.** at about 7 p.m.
07232 412119 (Paul)

2 Are these sentences true (T), (F) or the notices don't say (DS)?

1 [F] Mike wants more than £150 for his bike.

2 [ ] Anyone can apply for the job in Percy Street.

3 [ ] Carla is worried about losing all her notes.

4 [ ] This room will cost at least £90 every week.

5 [ ] The yoga class has eight lessons every two months.

6 [ ] The mobile phone was found by Paul.

Help with Writing Notices: abbreviations

3 **a)** We use some common abbreviations in notices. What do you think the abbreviations in **bold** mean in notices A–F?

Pls. = Please

b) Write the **bold** abbreviations in notices A–F next to their meaning.

1 per hour ......*p/h*......

2 non-smokers ....

3 very good condition ....

4 or near offer ....

5 per week ....

6 evenings ....

7 Tuesday ....

8 telephone number ....

c) Which other abbreviations do you know? Write these words/phrases next to their abbreviation.

~~Street~~	for example	Avenue	including
Thanks	April	as soon as possible	Road

1 St. ......*Street*......

2 Ave. ....

3 Apr. ....

4 e.g. ....

5 asap ....

6 incl. ....

7 Rd. ....

8 Thx. ....

4 Write notices for information a)–c). Use the abbreviations in **3** where possible.

a) Alex is offering a cookery course. There are 3-hour classes every week – on Saturday mornings. You can call him after 7 o'clock in the evening on 01923 434325.

Cookery course

b) Margie wants to rent out a double room in her house. It's £140 a week but that includes bills. She doesn't want anyone that smokes and you can email her on mjparks@ukmail.net.

c) Tom is selling his television. It's nearly new – he won it in a competition two months ago. He wants about £120 for it. The buyer will have to pick it up. He lives in Carston Avenue. His phone number is 07986 304207.

5 **a)** Think of something you would like to sell. Answer these questions and make notes.

What is it?

....

Is it in good condition?

....

How much is it? Will you take a near offer?

....

How should a buyer contact you?

....

When can they contact you?

....

b) Write a notice.

● Use your notes from **5a)**.
● Organise your notice and make it interesting.
● Use abbreviations.
● Read and check for mistakes.
● Give your notice to your teacher next class.

Tick the things you can do in English in the Reading and Writing Progress Portfolio, p88.

Holiday arrangements

Reading formal letters
Writing formal letters: American and British English
Review phrasal verbs (1): travel

 a) Are these sentences about formal letters true (T) or false (F)? Correct the false sentences.

1 [T] You should put your address first, before the address of the person you are writing to.

2 [　] A letter which starts *Dear Sir* should end *Yours faithfully*. A letter which starts *Dear Mr/Mrs*, etc. + surname should end *Yours sincerely*.

3 [　] The first paragraph of the letter should explain your reason for writing.

4 [　] You should start a new paragraph for each sentence.

5 [　] You should use contractions (*I'm*, *He's*, etc.).

6 [　] You should write your signature above your name.

b) Read letter A quickly. Which rule about formal letters in **1a)** <u>isn't</u> used in this letter?

 Read letter A again and choose the correct answer.

1 Where is Mr Turnbull's holiday?
a) Italy
b) the USA
c) The letter doesn't say.

2 Mr Turnbull will now set off …
a) earlier.
b) later.
c) at the same time.

3 Mr Turnbull is now staying at the hotel for …
a) seven nights.
b) more nights than before.
c) fewer nights than before.

4 They will now check out of the hotel on …
a) Friday.
b) Saturday.
c) Sunday.

5 Why has the hotel changed?
a) The original hotel is full.
b) The original hotel is closed for redecoration.
c) The letter doesn't say.

6 What is different about the new hotel?
a) It's not as good.
b) It's better.
c) It's nearer the airport.

7 How should Mr Turnbull get from the airport to the hotel?
a) Someone will pick him up.
b) He should get a taxi.
c) He should get a coach.

Color Blue Travel
14–18 Summer Street
MA 00105

12/17/06

15 Shaw Ave.
Bedford
MK40 2JA

Dear Mr Turnbull,

I am writing to inform you of some changes to your holiday arrangements in March 2007.

The flight will now leave at 10.15 a.m. on Saturday March 14th (03/14/07) not Friday March 13th (03/13/07). The hotel booking is still for 7 days and is therefore Saturday through Friday. The return flight is now Saturday March 21st (03/21/07). However, the hotel will now be Hotel Atlas. This hotel is a five-star hotel rather than the original three-star hotel offered.

Please note that all travelers will be taken from the airport to their hotel by a coach or taxi service.

We hope you are looking forward to your holiday with Color Blue Travel. We are very grateful for your cooperation with these changes and apologize for any inconvenience caused. Please contact us at the above address with any queries.

Sincerely,

Terry Samuels

Terry Samuels

Help with Writing Formal letters: American and British English

 3 **a)** Look at formal letter A in American English (US) and formal letter B in British English (UK). Starting formal letters in American and British English is the same. Complete the table for ending formal letters with *US* or *UK*.

ending a letter if you:

know the person's name	1 .... : Yours sincerely
	2 .... : Sincerely (yours)
don't know the person's name	3 .... : Yours faithfully
	4 *US* : Yours truly

b) Complete the table with examples of American English from letter A.

	British English	American English
dates	14th March 14/03/07	1 *March 14th* 2 ....
spelling	apologise colour traveller	3 .... 4 .... 5 ....
prepositions	Saturday to Friday	Saturday 6 .... Friday

---

(B)

Colour Blue Travel

14–18 Summer Street

MA 00105

21/12/06

15 Shaw Ave.

Bedford

MK40 2JA

Dear Mr Samuels,

Thank you for your letter with details of our changed holiday arrangements. We realise holiday arrangements sometimes have to change but the current flight times and hotel make our situation difficult. Firstly, we booked our original hotel to be near friends. Hotel Atlas is nearly 50 miles away from our original hotel. Secondly, we've got a relative's wedding on 14th March (14/03/07). We've been booking holidays with your company for over ten years and this is the first time we've been in this situation. I'd appreciate it if you could contact me on 00 44 1234 324732 to discuss this problem.

Yours sincerely,

Richard Turnbull

Richard Turnbull

 4 **a)** Read letter B. Richard Turnbull makes four common formal letter writing mistakes in his reply. What are they?

1 *You should put your address first.* ....

2 ....

3 ....

4 ....

b) Richard uses British English in his letter. Find four examples of British English and change them to American English. Use the tables in **3** to help you.

1 *Colour (UK) → Color (US)* 3 ....

2 .... 4 ....

5 **a)** Look at the following holiday arrangements. Make notes on your own ideas in the table.

	original	new
flight	04/10/07	
hotel	Hotel Luxor (***)	
other	pick-up service from airport	

b) Write either letter a) or letter b).

a) A letter from a travel company explaining the change in holiday arrangements.

b) A letter from a customer who has received these new arrangements but has a problem.

- Use your notes from **5a)**.
- Organise your letter correctly.
- Use either American English or British English.
- Read and check for mistakes.
- Give your letter to your teacher next class.

Tick the things you can do in English in the Reading and Writing Progress Portfolio, p88.

A book review

1 Read these reviews quickly. What connects the two books?

They are both:
a) written by journalists.   b) based on true stories.   c) about real people.

Reading book reviews
Writing book reviews: organisation, useful phrases
Review character adjectives; verb forms

books:reading:literature   REVIEWS

Cameron Crowe was once a teenage reporter for *Rolling Stone* – the famous American music magazine. He uses his experiences in his novel *Almost Famous* (Faber and Faber, £6.99). The main character is William Miller, a 15-year-old kid who is hired by *Rolling Stone* magazine to go on tour with an unknown band, Stillwater. Their adventures take place all over the USA as William learns about life and love. Crowe's writing is both interesting and believable.

The book also includes an interview with Cameron Crowe about his adventurous life and he explains some of the more confusing parts of the story.

You will not be disappointed by this book. The ending is thoughtful and emotional and I'm going to remember it for a long time.

In 1915 Henry James, the famous author, was seriously ill in his home in London. He was waiting to die. And this is where David Lodge's historical novel *Author! Author!* (Secker & Warburg, £6.99) begins. Lodge tells the story of Henry James' successes and failures in his novels and plays from *Portrait of a Lady* (recently a film with Nicole Kidman) to his disaster of a play *Guy Domville*. And *Author! Author!* would make an interesting historical film. The title itself is fantastic and refers to what audiences used to shout if they liked a play.

Lodge's novel is a sensitive story of an author who was never confident of his talent. And Henry James will get many more fans from people who read this book. I'm going to take a couple of his novels on holiday myself!

2 Read the reviews again and choose the best answer.

1 Cameron Crowe …
  a) was a journalist.
  b) was in a band.
  c) owned a magazine.

2 William goes on tour with …
  a) a famous group.
  b) The Rolling Stones.
  c) a new group.

3 The reviewer of *Almost Famous* particularly liked …
  a) the end of the story.
  b) the interview with Cameron Crowe.
  c) the title.

4 Henry James wrote …
  a) *Author! Author!*
  b) *Portrait of a Lady*.
  c) a book about Nicole Kidman.

5 The reviewer thinks *Author! Author!* …
  a) is a good play.
  b) should be made into a film.
  c) has a strange title.

6 On holiday the reviewer is going to read …
  a) *Author! Author!* again.
  b) some more David Lodge books.
  c) some more Henry James books.

Help with Writing Book reviews: organisation, useful phrases

 3 Both reviews in **1** contain four parts, which each have a different function. Put parts a)–d) in the order 1–4 in which they occur in the reviews.

a) Recommendation: ___4___

b) Plot: _____

c) Introduction to the story: _____

d) General comments: _____

4 The reviews use different verb forms for the different parts. Match parts a)–d) in **3** to 1–3.

1 past verb forms: ___c)___

2 present verb forms: _____ , _____

3 *will/be going to*: _____

5 The reviews contain some useful phrases for reviewing books. Match parts of the phrases 1–6 to a)–f) and then check your answers in the reviews.

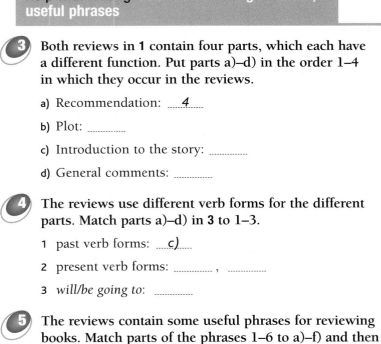

1 The book tells — a) character …
2 The main b) really good and refers to …
3 The title is c) a good film because …
4 The story takes d) is amazing/disappointing …
5 The ending e) the story of …
6 It would make f) place in …

6 Complete this review with the correct verb forms. Remember the four parts of a review in **3** and the different verb forms in **4**.

About 10 years ago I ¹ _went_ (go) skiing in Lahti, Finland. And this was the reason that *The Lahti File* by Richard MacAndrew (CUP, £3.50) ² _____ (attract) my attention. I ³ _____ also _____ (learn) English at the moment and this book is written especially for students. The novel ⁴ _____ (take) place in Finland and MacAndrew ⁵ _____ (describe) the town of Lahti very well. The main character ⁶ _____ (be) a spy called Ian Munro. He's sent to Lahti to investigate several strange deaths.

The book ⁷ _____ (be) also available on CD and if you want to practise your English more, there ⁸ _____ (be) worksheets on CUP's website.

If you like a good thriller, you ⁹ _____ (love) *The Lahti File*. The ending is very exciting and I have a feeling there are going to be more novels with Ian Munro. I ¹⁰ _____ (read) them all!

 7 Rewrite these sentences using the word in brackets.

1 At the end the story is amazing. (ending)
   The ending is amazing. _____

2 The book is about a young boy who has no parents. (tells) _____
   _____

3 The most important person in the book is Jack. (main) _____
   _____

4 The story happens in Buenos Aires, Argentina. (place) _____
   _____

5 I think a film version would be good because the book is so exciting. (make) _____
   _____

6 The name of the book is *Loyal* because of the relationship between the man and his dog (title; refer) _____
   _____

 8 a) Think about a book you have read recently and make notes in the table.

title of the book	
some background information	
takes place	
main character	
general comments	
recommendation	

b) Write a review of your book.

- Use your notes from **8a)**.
- Organise your review and use the verb forms in **4**.
- Use the phrases in **5**.
- Read and check for mistakes.
- Give your review to your teacher next class.

Tick the things you can do in English in the Reading and Writing Progress Portfolio, p88.

Emails with news

Reading an informal email
Writing short emails and notes: useful phrases
Review verb patterns; homes

1 Read the email and fill in gaps 1–8 with the correct words.

1 a) absolutely
  b) very
  c) fairly

2 a) more far
  b) more further
  c) further

3 a) read
  b) 'd read
  c) 've read

4 a) to pack
  b) packing
  c) pack

5 a) enough big
  b) big enough
  c) enough room

6 a) B&Bs
  b) airports
  c) stations

7 a) flights
  b) planes
  c) flying

8 a) thinks
  b) thinking
  c) think

From: alex@rousso.co.uk
To: huwprice@medaid.com; arvind@24-7work.com; (plus 10 others...)
Subject: Greetings from Scotland!

Hi everyone,

We've finally moved! The house is ¹ _absolutely_ gorgeous – better than I remember it. And the cat's fascinated by the garden – she was born in our old flat and she's never been ² _____ than the balcony!

We're so grateful for all your cards and presents. I ³ _____ the cards again this morning and they made me cry! (Can anyone tell me what Pat Austin's email is? She sent some flowers to our new address.)

We're so sorry that we didn't come to Jackie and Bill's party on Saturday afternoon. What happened was that we were supposed to finish ⁴ _____ in the afternoon. But we quickly realised the lorry wasn't ⁵ _____ . So in the end we had to hire another van and Mike had to drive to Edinburgh in the evening.

Talking of parties, we're going to have a house-warming party on 3rd February. Would you all like to come? I know it'll be a long time after we've moved in but we might have a chance to decorate first. We'd rather get organised before you come! I'm telling you about this more than three months in advance so there are no excuses. There are lots of ⁶ _____ nearby and some of you can sleep here. Don't forget to book train or plane tickets soon if you're going to come! Superflights (www.superflights.com) are offering ⁷ _____ to Edinburgh for £30 at the moment but they'll get more expensive soon.

Everything's still in boxes of course, but I don't start work for a week. Lucien's got an interview next week so ⁸ _____ of him on Wednesday.

Anyway, more news soon. Hope you all have a lovely break during the holiday!

Much love,

Alex (and Lucien)

---

2 Read the email again. Are these sentences true (T) or false (F)?

1 [T] Alex and Lucien's cat had never been outside before.
2 [ ] Alex wants to find out where Pat Austin lives.
3 [ ] They didn't go to the party because they were tired.
4 [ ] They're having a party at their new house next year.
5 [ ] Their new house has enough space for some guests to stay.
6 [ ] It's a good idea to book train or plane tickets to Edinburgh in advance.
7 [ ] Alex and Lucien moved because Lucien has got a new job.

Help with Writing
Short emails and notes: useful phrases

3 **a)** Find phrases 1–8 in the letter and <u>underline</u> them.

1 We'd rather …
2 We're so sorry that …
3 Don't forget …
4 Can anyone tell me … ?
5 Hope you have …
6 We're so grateful for …
7 What happened was that …
8 Would you like … ?

b) Match phrases 1–8 in **3a)** with meanings a)–h).

a) [2] apologising
b) [ ] reminding
c) [ ] wishing someone a good thing
d) [ ] thanking
e) [ ] inviting someone
f) [ ] saying your preference
g) [ ] explaining what happened
h) [ ] asking for information

c) Which phrase or phrases in **3a)** are often followed by:

a) an infinitive _____
b) an infinitive with *to* _____ , _____

4 **a) Complete these sentences with phrases 1–8 in 3a).**

1 _We're so sorry that_ we didn't do the washing-up. I promise I'll do it when I get home.

2 .... a good time at the gig. I'd love to come but I've got to work tonight.

3 .... if this is rubbish? I'd like to get rid of it.

4 A Have you decided how you're getting to Alex's party?

B .... fly than get the train.

5 .... your help last Saturday. You must be as tired as we are today.

6 .... to meet me for lunch tomorrow? I've got a meeting near your office and it finishes at about one o'clock.

7 I didn't tell you why we left early on Friday, did I? .... I got a phone call from the babysitter.

8 .... to ring your mum. She called yesterday.

b) Read the situations and write sentences using the correct form of the phrases in 3a).

1 You have just arrived at the cinema. You are meeting a friend and you are late because you couldn't find your keys. **Apologise** to your friend and **explain** what happened.

I'm so sorry that I'm late. What happened was that

I couldn't find my keys.

2 It's your parents' wedding anniversary tomorrow. **Remind** your brother.

....

....

....

3 You are looking for the station but you are lost. **Ask** a group of people.

....

....

....

4 You received a birthday present from friends who are going on holiday tomorrow. **Thank** them for the present and **wish** them a good time on holiday.

....

....

....

5 You want to go to a pop concert on Friday. **Invite** your friend and say you **prefer** going with someone rather than going alone.

....

....

....

5 **a) Match situations 1–3 to plans a)–c) for a short email.**

1 You borrowed a friend's CD and broke it.

....

2 You had dinner at a friend's house on Friday.

....

3 Your boss is going on holiday next week.

....

a) ● thank your friend.
   ● invite your friend to go out next week.
   ● remind your friend to bring your jacket you left at his/her house.

b) ● say you'd prefer to work at home on Friday.
   ● ask him/her for his mobile number in case of emergency.
   ● wish him/her a good time.

c) ● apologise for the accident.
   ● explain what happened.
   ● say what you're going to do.

b) Write three short emails for situations 1–3 in 5a).

● Use the plans in **5a)**.
● Use the phrases in **3a)**.
● Read and check for mistakes.
● Give your emails to your teacher next class.

Tick the things you can do in English in the Reading and Writing Progress Portfolio, p88.

Letters to a newspaper

Reading an article and two letters about pocket money
Writing giving an opinion
Review conditionals; *make* and *do*

1 Read the article and letters quickly. Who:

a) thinks children should work for their pocket money? ....

b) isn't sure if children should work for their pocket money? ....

c) disagrees with a)? ....

Househusband

By Phil Marsden

Pocket money – do your kids earn it?

I have three children who are 8, 10 and 12. They get pocket money every Saturday of between £3 and £5. This is about the national British average but according to a recent survey, British children receive the highest pocket money in Europe. And of course, <u>they're absolutely convinced that</u> their friends get at least twice as much as they do.

I've always felt that pocket money is a good idea. I have no doubt that it teaches children to think about money and to save up for things they want –

appropriate training for adult life. However, recently we've started to ask our kids to earn their pocket money. They do the washing-up, for example, or do some cleaning. Or sometimes we pay them not to make noise!

They're not happy about it! They say that they don't have time. They say their friends don't have to do anything for their pocket money. My twelve-year-old makes me laugh. As far as he's concerned, we pay less than the government's minimum wage! When he refused to help my wife do the shopping recently, we didn't give him his pocket money for a week. He was so upset that we had to have a family meeting to discuss the situation. (And then later I saw our eight-year-old gave him half of *her* pocket money!)

So what do you think readers? We're not being unfair, are we?

We've got two children. They started getting pocket money when they were about four. But it was always for helping or doing some work. Now, they're 14 and 16 and they volunteer to make dinner and do the housework. As they see it, they have to earn their pocket money.

I'm positive that your own children will soon learn the same thing. And if they refuse, don't give them their pocket money!

Children who are old enough – and yours are – have to learn that home is not a hotel!

Barry, North London

To me, children are becoming obsessed by money – just like their parents! If you give children money for helping at home, then they start thinking they should make money out of anything and everything they do.

We have four boys (2, 7, 9 and 13). The three who receive pocket money get it every week on Saturday morning. It doesn't matter how much work they have done or what they have done at school. Of course, we ask them to help at home. And *usually* they do everything we ask them to do. And if they don't do it, there is usually a good reason. If there isn't one, we'll tell them that we're disappointed. We strongly believe that this is a much better idea than the threat of no pocket money.

Nicole, Glasgow

2 Read the article and letters again. Are these sentences true (T), false (F) or the text doesn't say (DS)?

1 | F | Phil has always asked his children to help around the house.

2 | | Phil thinks pocket money is important because children learn about saving money.

3 | | Phil's eldest child never helps with the housework.

4 | | Phil gives his children extra money for doing things in the house.

5 | | Barry's children expect to help at home.

6 | | Barry thinks Phil's children should help at home.

7 | | Nicole gives pocket money to her four children.

8 | | Nicole's children always help her when they can.

9 | | Nicole's children don't mind doing the housework.

3 Each letter is organised into three paragraphs. Match paragraphs A–F to functions 1–3.

1 Further details about the problem:

   ....*A*...... , ...

2 Suggestion of a solution:

   .... , ...

3 Introduction to the problem:

   .... , ...

4 **a)** The letters are formal and use connecting words. Which connecting words in **bold** are similar in meaning to *and* or *but*?

1 and: *In addition* , ... ,

   ....

2 but: .... , ... ,

   ....

b) Complete these rules with the connecting words in **4a)**.

1 We use *although* or ....
   to contrast two clauses in the same
   sentence.

2 We use .... to contrast
   two sentences. (We always put a
   comma after this word.)

3 We use .... ,
   .... or .... at
   the beginning of sentences to add
   more information.

5 **a)** Formal letters often use the passive. <u>Underline</u> examples of the passive in the letters.

b) Why is the passive used in the letters? Tick the correct reasons.

1 ☐ The subject isn't important.

2 ☐ We want to keep the subject secret.

3 ☐ The subject is obvious.

4 ☐ We don't know the subject.

6 Choose the correct words. Sometimes both answers are possible.

1 The park is empty in the week. *Moreover/*(*However*), it is quite crowded at weekends.

2 *Even though/However*, there is a lot of traffic, I love where I live.

3 Schools are not teaching students about recycling. *Furthermore/ Even though* there are very few recycling bins in our town.

4 *Even though/Although* I recycle a lot of rubbish, I know I could do more.

5 There is nothing to do in our town at weekends. *Moreover/ However*, there are very few places to go at night.

6 There aren't many places to park here. *In addition/Furthermore* the car parks we have are incredibly expensive.

7 The British recycle about 12% of their rubbish. *Furthermore/ However*, the Japanese recycle over 40% of theirs.

7 Write these sentences in the passive.

1 They've put in more cycle lanes. *More cycle lanes have been put in.*

2 They must repair the road. _____

3 People don't use recycling bins regularly.

   _____

4 No one ever empties the bins. _____

5 They recycle a lot of glass. _____

6 They told me that they would replace the lights.

   _____

8 **a)** Think about a problem in your town or city. Make notes in the table.

describe the problem	
further details about the problem	
possible solutions	
possible results	

b) Write a formal letter to a local newspaper about the problem you chose in **8a)**.

- Use your notes from **8a)**.
- Use the organisation of the letter in **3**.
- Use the connecting words in **4** where possible.
- Use the passive if appropriate.
- Read and check for mistakes.
- Give your letter to your teacher next class.

> Tick the things you can do in English in the Reading and Writing Progress Portfolio, p88.

A letter of application

Reading a job advertisement; a letter of application
Writing letters of application: organisation, useful phrases
Review work collocations

1 Read the advertisement. Tick four more qualities you think an applicant for this job should have.

a) organised ✓
b) speaks foreign languages
c) gets on well with people
d) ability to work overtime
e) good computer skills
f) non-smoker
g) ability to make quick decisions
h) ability to drive

2 Read the letter of application and answer the questions.

1 Where did Christine see the advertisement?

  In the Guardian newspaper.

2 Does Christine ever teach at the Black Lion? ....

3 What information in the advertisement does Christine talk about in her letter? ....
....

4 Why does she want a new job?
....
....
....
....

5 How do we know Christine likes doing sport? ....
....

6 What has Christine sent with her application letter? ....

7 What kind of person do you think Christine is? ....
....
....

Fitness Trainer

We require an experienced fitness trainer for the Well Retreat Centre. As part of a team, you will develop training programmes for our customers. You will travel to several of our centres and give advice and training to other Well Retreat Centre instructors. This position is based at our centre in North London but involves extensive travel and flexible working hours.

Please apply in writing with a recent CV to:

Dear Sir/Madam,

A [1]I am writing in reply to your advertisement in the *Guardian* for a fitness trainer at the Well Retreat Centre.

B [2]At the moment, I am working as the Health and Fitness assistant manager at the Black Lion Sports Centre in Kent. [3]My responsibilities range from organising timetables and managing instructors to giving classes. I also offer specialised fitness training advice for several gyms in London and in the Southeast. This role involves working with instructors and customers to plan diets, fitness and lifestyle programmes, according to their needs. I work long hours, but I enjoy my work.

C I have been working at the Black Lion and for other gyms for three years and both jobs have taught me a wide range of skills that are valuable in my work. However, I would now like the opportunity to develop these skills in a full-time position with more responsibility. Furthermore, I would also like to work in more of a team environment. For these reasons [4]I am very interested in working for the Well Retreat Centre.

D [5]As you will see from my CV, fitness is also one of my main interests. When I have time to relax, I go running. I recently participated in this year's London Marathon. I have also written several articles for fitness training magazines in the UK and the USA.

E I would be pleased to discuss this letter and my enclosed CV, and [6]I look forward to hearing from you.

Yours faithfully,

Christine Paine
Christine Paine

Help with Writing Letters of application: organisation

3 Read the letter again. Match paragraphs A–E to functions 1–5.

1 Further information about yourself: *D*   3 Conclusion: ......   5 Why you are applying: ......

2 What you are doing at the moment: ......   4 Why you are writing: ......

Help with Writing Letters of application: useful phrases

4 **a)** Look at the formal phrases 1–6 in **bold** in the letter. Match them to informal sentences a)–f).

a) There is some information about this on my CV. ___5___

b) I saw your advert in the paper so I thought I'd write. _____

c) I really want to work for your company. _____

d) These are the things I have to do at work. _____

e) Please write soon. _____

f) This is what I do now. _____

b) Complete phrases 1–6 from the letter with these words.

| ~~in~~   at   as (x 2)   from (x 3)   in (x 2)   to (x 3)   for (x 2) |

1 I am writing __in__ reply _____ your advertisement _____ the *Guardian* _____ a ...

2 _____ the moment, I am working _____ a/the ...

3 My responsibilities range _____ ... _____ ...

4 I am very interested _____ working _____ ...

5 _____ you will see _____ my CV, ...

6 I look forward _____ hearing _____ you.

5 **a)** Read this letter of application. Put paragraphs A–E in the correct order.

___D___ , _____ , _____ , _____ , _____

A
At the moment I am working full-time at a receptionist for a large American bank in London. My responsibilities range of meeting visitors to answering phones and taking messages.

B
I look forward to hearing of you.
Yours sincerely,
Elizabeth West
Elizabeth West

C
I am interested of medical issues and three years ago, I had a temporary position with a secretary on the Wellington Hospital. I believe my experience, interest and enthusiasm would be excellent for your position.

D
Dear Mrs Crouch,
I am writing the reply to your advertisement on *The Times* of a receptionist at St John's Wood Surgery.

E
As you will see on my CV, I have over nine years of experience. In this time, I have learned a wide variety of skills connected with my work. I have also realised that I particularly enjoy the personal contact that receptionists have with people. Therefore I would like the opportunity to work in a smaller office environment.

b) Read the letter of application again. Find ten mistakes and correct them.

6 **a)** Choose one of these advertisements or your own idea. Make notes on a letter of application in the table.

Personal trainers

Our agency has a personal trainer position available. You will be working with musicians on tours all over the world. You should have at least 5 years of experience of fitness training and diet planning.

Santé Health Centre

We are looking for a cook for our health centre in Wallingford, near Oxford. We run courses for people who are following special diets as part of a health programme. You should have experience and lots of ideas about cooking for special diets.

where you saw the advertisement	
what you are doing at the moment	
why you are applying	
further information about yourself	

b) Write a letter of application.

- Use your notes from **6a)**.
- Use the organisation of the letter in **3**.
- Use the formal phrases in **4**.
- Read and check for mistakes.
- Give your letter to your teacher next class.

Tick the things you can do in English in the Reading and Writing Progress Portfolio, p88.

Describing people

Reading a description of a good friend
Writing descriptions of people: organisation, useful phrases
Review describing people; character adjectives; adjectives to describe behaviour

1 Read the description quickly. Tick the things 1–5 that Fiona mentions.

1 ☐ Kate's boyfriend.

2 ☐ How Fiona met Kate.

3 ☐ Kate's personality.

4 ☐ Kate's appearance.

5 ☐ Kate's favourite hobbies.

About six years ago I was invited to an old school friend's wedding. We had been really good friends at school but I hadn't seen her for a few years. So I was a bit surprised to get an invitation. When I realised I knew no one else at the wedding, I thought it was going to be a long day ... But then I met Kate. And, well, I guess she's my best friend now.

The first thing I noticed about Kate was her shoes. In fact it was difficult to miss them! They were bright red and they were the only thing I could see – she was under a table looking for her contact lens! As I walked by I said, "Nice shoes!" and I heard her say, "Thanks!" Then, when she came out from under the table we looked at each other and laughed! We had exactly the same dress on! We have very similar taste in clothes in fact – we like bright clothes – striped and flowery dresses and tops. But we look completely different. She is tanned and looks Spanish or Italian. I look typically English! We're both in our mid-twenties but my hair is short and blonde and hers is long and dark. I'm not very tall but she's taller than most men I know. In fact, she looks like a model and I ... well, I don't!

Our personalities are very different, too. She's much more confident than I am. But she can be so disorganised at times. I can't remember the number of times we've missed the start of a film, play or concert because Kate was late! However, she's funny, warm and the most considerate and unselfish person I know. She's always ready with a cup of tea and some good advice when I have a problem.

I've learned so much from Kate. And I was so lucky to meet her. I'm sure we'll be friends for life. And all because of those lovely red shoes and her great taste in clothes!

2 Read the description again and answer these questions.

1 Where did Fiona meet Kate?

....

2 Why did they start talking?

....

3 What kind of things do they both like?

....

4 How are they different in appearance?

....

....

....

....

....

5 How are they different in personality?

....

....

....

6 Why does Fiona think Kate is kind?

....

....

....

Help with Writing Descriptions of people: organisation, useful phrases

3 Fiona's story contains four parts, which each have a different function. Put parts a)–d) in the order 1–4 in which they occur in the description.

a) Her feelings now: ___4___

b) Character: _____

c) Introduction/How they met: _____

d) Physical appearance/Clothes: _____

4 **a)** Read the description again. <u>Underline</u> these useful phrases for describing people.

1 We have similar taste in ...
2 I/We look ...
3 She looks like a ...
4 She's the ... (person) I know.

b) Which phrase or phrases in **4a)**:

a) are followed by a noun? ___1___ , _____

b) contains a superlative? _____

c) is followed by an adjective? _____

5 **a)** Complete sentence b) so it has the same meaning as sentence a). Use the phrases in **4a)**.

1 **a)** She has a worried expression on her face.

 b) *She looks worried.*

2 **a)** People think I'm intelligent because I wear glasses!

 b) I _____ because I wear glasses!

3 **a)** We like the same kind of music.

 b) We have _____ music.

4 **a)** Can you tell me about her appearance?

 b) Can you tell me what she

 _____ ?

5 **a)** I don't know anyone more talented than Paul.

 b) Paul is _____ person I know.

6 **a)** Jean and Kate enjoy the same type of films.

 b) Jean and Kate have _____ films.

7 **a)** I have a similar face to my sister.

 b) I look _____ sister.

8 **a)** I don't know anyone worse at driving than him.

 b) He _____ driver I know.

b) Correct the mistakes in these sentences.

 angry
1 They look ~~angrily~~, don't they?

2 My brother and I have similar taste on cars.

3 People think I look like Swedish but I'm actually Brazilian!

4 My dad is one of the most funny people I know.

5 He looks likes his father, doesn't he?

6 She looks well in that dress.

6 **a)** Think about someone you know well. Make notes in the table.

how you met	
physical appearance	
personality	
what you think of the person now	

b) Write a description.

● Use your notes from **6a)**.
● Use the organisation of the description in **3**.
● Use the phrases in **4**.
● Read and check for mistakes.
● Give your description to your teacher next class.

Tick the things you can do in English in the Reading and Writing Progress Portfolio, p88.

Telling a story

Reading a story about an interview
Writing verb forms in stories
Review Past Simple; Past Continuous; Past Perfect

When Jamie walked into the offices of the Charlton Corporation, he was feeling absolutely terrified. He'd never been in such a large building before. Everything looked so clean, so organised and even quite glamorous. It didn't help, of course, that he was late. He'd decided to go by underground rather than the bus and it'd been delayed. He'd sat in a tunnel near Paddington Station. He hadn't even been able to use his mobile to tell them he'd be late.

It was now 9.25 and his interview was supposed to start at 9.

He told the receptionist his name and apologised for being late. The receptionist told him not to worry. In fact, he told Jamie, one of the interviewers hadn't arrived yet. So it didn't matter. Jamie sat down in one of the large armchairs in reception and picked up a newspaper. But he couldn't concentrate on any of the stories.

"Relax, Jamie. Relax," he told himself.

About five minutes later a woman sat down beside Jamie. She was wearing a suit and carrying a leather bag that looked expensive. She looked nervous too.

"Nice bag," Jamie said.

"Thank you," she replied. "Are you here for an interview?"

Jamie suddenly felt a lot better. She was obviously in the same situation as he was. And she was quite good-looking, too.

"Yes," he said.

"Are you feeling nervous?" she asked.

"No, not really," Jamie lied. "Although an old school friend of mine works here and he says that my interviewer is really bad-tempered and rude. She works in a different office and every time he's met her, she's been really arrogant. So I'm not looking forward to that!"

The woman laughed. She had a beautiful laugh, Jamie thought. They started chatting about interviews. Jamie told her about the time he'd gone for an interview and realised he still had a piece of chewing gum in his mouth. He'd been so nervous that he'd put it under his chair in the interview room. She laughed again. She likes me, Jamie thought.

He told the woman some more stories about himself. He lost his last permanent job, he told her, when he fell asleep at his desk the day after a big party at a friend's house. He hadn't really cared as he thought the job was too stressful anyway. She laughed again. Maybe he should ask her for her phone number, Jamie thought.

1

Read the first part of the story and put events a)–h) in the correct order 1–6. There are two extra events that do <u>not</u> happen in the story.

a) **1** Jamie put some chewing gum under a chair.

b) ☐ Jamie said sorry to the receptionist.

c) ☐ The woman and Jamie talked about interviews.

d) ☐ Jamie caught an underground train.

e) ☐ The woman told Jamie she had an interview too.

f) ☐ Jamie asked the woman for her phone number.

g) ☐ Jamie arrived at the Charlton Corporation.

h) ☐ Jamie met the woman.

2

Read the story again and choose the best answers.

1 Why was Jamie nervous?
   a) Because he had an interview.
   b) Because he was late.
   c) Both a) and b).

2 How was Jamie lucky?
   a) One of his interviewers was also late.
   b) His underground train wasn't delayed for long.
   c) No one else had applied for the job.

3 Why did Jamie lie to the woman?
   a) Because he was feeling more relaxed.
   b) Because he thought the woman was nervous.
   c) Because he thought she was attractive.

4 How did Jamie know something about his interviewer?
   a) He had worked with her before.
   b) One of his friends knew her.
   c) He had been at school with her.

5 Why did Jamie think the woman liked him?
   a) Because she laughed at all his stories.
   b) Because she told him she did.
   c) Both a) and b).

Help with Writing Verb forms in stories

 3 **a)** <u>Underline</u> the first example of each of these verb forms in the first part of the story.

1 Present Perfect Simple *he's met*
2 Past Simple
3 Past Continuous
4 Past Perfect
5 Present Simple
6 Present Continuous

b) Look at where the verb forms are used and choose the correct word in the rules.

● We usually use *present/past* verb forms in direct speech in stories.
● We usually use *present/past* verb forms in stories when we describe things that happen.

c) Look at the story again. Which verb forms are used most often in the story?

4 **a)** Read and complete the second part of the story with the correct form of the verb in brackets.

At that moment, a man appeared and Jamie's new friend ¹ _stood_ (stand) up. The man ² _____ obviously _____ (meet) the woman before. They kissed each other on the cheek and Jamie, stupidly, felt a bit jealous. But while they ³ _____ (walk) towards the lift, the woman looked back, ⁴ _____ (smile) and said "Good luck!"

A few minutes later, the receptionist told Jamie that his interviewers were ready now. He took Jamie to a room at the end of a long corridor and ⁵ _____ (knock) on the door.

Two people ⁶ _____ (talk) in the room and Jamie heard someone laugh.

Then the receptionist opened the door and looked at Jamie.

"⁷ _____ you _____ (feel) OK?" the receptionist asked.

Jamie's face ⁸ _____ (be) white. He suddenly felt sick. He ⁹ _____ (hear) that laugh before. And although he ¹⁰ _____ (not can) see his interviewers yet, he could see a familiar expensive leather bag on the table ...

b) Why didn't Jamie feel very well when he arrived at the room?

_____

_____

5 **a)** Think about a time you felt very nervous about something, for example an interview or your first day at a new school or work place. Make notes in the table.

What was the day?	
How did you feel? Why?	
Did you meet anyone who helped you feel less nervous?	
What happened in the end?	

b) Write a story about your experience.

● Use your notes from **5a)**.
● Use past verb forms (Past Simple, Past Perfect, etc.) to describe the things that happened and, if necessary, present verb forms (Present Simple, etc.) for direct speech.
● Remember that you can invent some or all of the story if you want to.
● Read and check for mistakes.
● Give your story to your teacher next class.

Tick the things you can do in English in the Reading and Writing Progress Portfolio, p88.

Describing important moments

Reading descriptions of important moments
Writing common mistakes; descriptions of events
Review work collocations; phrasal verbs for travel

The day that changed my life

ALL WEEK, we've been collecting your stories on important moments. We've had stories from all over the world – some romantic, some funny, some sad. **a)Here are a few of the best.**

Ten years ago, I was in my final year at university. During the holidays I decided to visit my grandparents, who live in Boston, USA. **b)I was waiting in the queue at Heathrow check-in when a woman approached me.** She worked for the airline and she told me that they had overbooked the flight. She offered me a flight anywhere in Europe if I agreed to take a later flight to Boston. My grandparents wouldn't worry and I wasn't in a hurry so I agreed.

When I got home from my grandparents, I started thinking about my free flight. Paris, perhaps? A weekend in Venice or Barcelona?

A few nights later, I got a phone call from an old friend, Owen. We'd known each other at university but he was a year older than me. When he'd left university, we'd lost touch. Anyway, he was teaching in Lisbon, Portugal. We chatted for a long time, so I decided to go and see him.

He had only been in Lisbon for a year but his Portuguese seemed really good. I was impressed. **c)And I don't know if it was his language skills, the sunshine or Lisbon itself.** But on that short visit I fell in love with Owen. Three years ago we got married. And in November, we're going to have a baby. **d)If I hadn't agreed to take a later flight, I might never have met Owen again!**

Mia, Maida Vale, London

Five years ago I was working in an office. **e)My life was all about dealing with complaints,** meeting deadlines and writing reports. I wasn't completely bored but it didn't excite me. One lunchtime I went out to buy a sandwich. It was sunny and I wasn't busy at work so I decided to eat it in the park. I could see a group of people filming a TV programme nearby. They seemed to be arguing about something and everybody looked very stressed.

Suddenly I realised **f)everyone was looking at me.** And then two of them starting walking over – towards me! They explained that they were making a short film and one of their actors hadn't turned up. He only had one line in the story, they said. Would I mind saying the line?

I could tell they were desperate and although I'd never done any acting in my life, for some reason I agreed.

An hour later we had finished. **g)It had been an amazing experience.** The people were very grateful and paid me for my time. However, as I was leaving, the director of the film came over and gave me his card. He thought I'd been brilliant and was naturally talented as an actor. I laughed but promised to call him some time.

Well, I did call him. And I went for an audition for another short film with the director. And I got the job. Two years later I left my office job and I'm now working almost full-time as an actor. **h)I love the work** and I'm going back to college next year to study drama. My life is now completely different. And all because of lunch in the park!

Steven, St. John's Wood, London

1 Read the article quickly. Whose description is connected with:

a) his/her career? ....

b) a relationship? ....

2 Read the descriptions again. Are these sentences true (T), false (F) or doesn't the article say (DS)?

1 [F] Mia was offered a free flight because the flight to Boston was cancelled.

2 [   ] Owen and Mia went out at university.

3 [   ] Owen wasn't Portuguese.

4 [   ] Mia was still studying at university when she first went to Portugal.

5 [   ] Steven hated his old job.

6 [   ] Steven had always wanted to be an actor.

7 [   ] He got some money for his first job as an actor.

8 [   ] He left work because he had too much acting work.

3 Choose the reasons which probably helped Mia or Steven to make the decision that changed their life. Write M (Mia), S (Steven) or B (both) next to each reason.

a) family ...M...

b) the weather ....

c) time ....

d) something free ....

e) boredom ....

Help with Writing Common mistakes

 4 **a)** Students often make mistakes in language areas 1–8 when they write. Look at phrases a)–h) in **bold** in the article. Match a)–h) to 1–8.

1 same sound but different spelling (*here/hear, they're/there, you're/your*, etc.) a)

2 Present Simple/Present Continuous with state verbs (*like, hate*, etc.): _____

3 Past Simple/Past Continuous in sentences with *when/while*: _____

4 *everyone* + third person: _____

5 reflexive pronouns: _____

6 commonly confused nouns or verbs, (*experience/experiment, argue/discuss, make/do*, etc.): _____

7 verbs + prepositions (*deal with*, etc.): _____

8 conditional sentences: _____

b) Match language areas 1–8 in **4a)** with these examples of correct and incorrect sentences.

a) [5] *I'm teaching myself to play the piano.*

not ~~I'm teaching me to play the piano~~.

b) [ ] *I heard you're getting married soon.*

not ~~I heard your getting married soon~~.

c) [ ] *If I'd been on time, we wouldn't have been late.*

not ~~If I wouldn't have been late, ...~~

d) [ ] *Can you deal with a customer complaint?*

not ~~Can you deal of a customer complaint?~~

e) [ ] *I was waiting for a bus when I met her.*

not ~~I waited for a bus when I met her~~.

f) [ ] *Everyone wants to meet you.*

not ~~Everyone want to meet you~~.

g) [ ] *My brother and I very often argue.*

not ~~My brother and I very often discuss~~.

h) [ ] *I love my job.*

not ~~I'm loving my job~~.

5 Read these descriptions of important moments. Find four more mistakes in each one and correct them.

> *myself*
> I hate writing about ~~me~~ but I wanted to say something on this topic. The day that changed my life is not connected with luck or serendipity. It's simply the day my daughter was born. Everyone say that babies change your life. And there right! I don't get as much sleep as I used to. And I don't go out as much. But every day I'm thinking how lucky I am to be a father. And I can't believe that I didn't do this decision years ago.
>
> *Pete Kenny, West Hampstead, London*

> My moment is rather silly really. But it's important to me. About five years ago I woke up one morning and decided I couldn't go to work that day. I phoned my boss and told her I wasn't well. Then, I lay in bed, thinking in my life. "You need a cup of tea," I told myself. But while I made it, I knocked over the milk. If there is one thing I can't stand, it's tea without milk. So I walked, in a miserable mood, to the corner shop to buy some. Back at home, I noticed a competition on the outside of the milk carton. I can't even remember what I had to do now. Anyway, I entered the competition and ... I won! Two weeks' holiday for myself and a friend in the Caribbean. Not much I know, but at the time I really needed that holiday. And if I wouldn't have had it, I wouldn't have made several important decisions that changed my life.
>
> *Kate Barker, Kilburn, London*

 6 **a)** Think about an important moment in your life so far. Make notes in the table.

What happened?	
What were you doing at the time?	
How did it change your life?	

b) Write a description about your important moment.

- Use your notes in **6a)**.
- Remember that you can invent some or all of your description.
- Read and check for the common mistakes in **4**.
- Write your description again if you need to.
- Give your description to your teacher next class.

Tick the things you can do in English in the Reading and Writing Progress Portfolio, p88.

Intermediate Reading and Writing Progress Portfolio

Tick the things you can do in English.

Portfolio	Reading	Writing
1 p64	☐ I can understand a simple personal letter talking about a holiday. ☐ I can understand descriptions of events in private letters.	☐ I can write a letter expressing my experiences and feelings about a holiday. ☐ I can use and understand ellipsis of words in informal writing.
2 p66	☐ I can understand notices and common abbreviations used in them.	☐ I can write a detailed notice using appropriate abbreviations.
3 p68	☐ I can understand formal letters and detailed information given in them.	☐ I can write a formal letter and use simple British or American English appropriately.
4 p70	☐ I can read a book review and understand the main information and the reviewer's opinion.	☐ I can write a book review that is clearly organised and uses appropriate language.
5 p72	☐ I can read emails which talk about everyday life, and understand the facts and the reasons why people are writing.	☐ I can write a detailed personal letter describing experiences, feelings and events. ☐ I can use appropriate language for a wide variety of functions, including apologising, thanking and asking for information.
6 p74	☐ I can read columns in newspapers in which someone has an opinion on a topic.	☐ I can write an article which expresses my opinion on a subject using appropriate language.
7 p76	☐ I can understand simple technical instructions for everyday equipment.	☐ I can write clear, organised instructions and use appropriate connecting words.
8 p78	☐ I can understand the main points in short letters to a newspaper about current and familiar topics.	☐ I can write a letter on a problem in my local area. ☐ I can use appropriate connecting words for linking sentences and paragraphs.
9 p80	☐ I can read and understand the most important points in a job advertisement.	☐ I can reply in written form to job advertisements using appropriate language and style.
10 p82	☐ I can understand a detailed description of a person's appearance and personality.	☐ I can write a description of a friend using appropriate language and phrases.
11 p84	☐ I can understand the plot of a clearly organised story and recognise what the most important events are.	☐ I can write about real or fictional events and experiences using appropriate verb forms.
12 p86	☐ I can understand in a story the reasons for characters' actions and their results.	☐ I can monitor and correct common mistakes in my writing. ☐ I can write a description of an event – real or imagined – and use appropriate verb forms.